"Taylor-Hough's recipes are easy, with a minimum amount of ingredients and labor. And she presents the plan with an eye toward flexibility, allowing cooks to adapt the freeze-ahead plan to their own palates and checkbooks."

—*Johnson City Press*, Tennessee

"Offers kid-tested recipes that are easy and affordable."

—*The Oregonian*

"Cooks looking to save time without resorting to expensive convenience food will find this book helpful."

—*Herald-Journal*

"[This] book outlines a step-by-step plan to one dedicated day in the kitchen that will provide breakfasts, lunches and dinners for the following month."

—*Detroit News*

"A cookbook well worth a second look."

—*The Pilot*, North Carolina

"Just about everyone will find the planning and organizational tips valuable."

—*The Light Connection*

"The book is a one-stop resource for those looking to increase their time at the family table and decrease time spent in the kitchen and drive-through lanes."

—*The Cookbook Collectors' Exchange*

Praise fo

"*Frozen Assets* will prove to be the _____ cooking."

—Susan R. Sands, publisher, *Home Words* Magazine

"This book offers relief to those tired of eating restaurant fare or expensive, over-packaged convenience foods at the end of a hard day. Recommended…"

—*Library Journal*

"Contains recipe ideas, plus detailed instructions on how to get the maximum value from your food doll___ ___ ___ reparation times. If you are _____ our culinary life, this book _____

—Amazon.com

"Finally, a _____ f cooking from scratch wit_____

—_____thly Newsletter

"This cookb_____ money while still providi_____

—_____ing Magazine

"This title is t_____ _____sive scope and easygoing sty_____

—*Christian Parenting Today*

"Hate to cook? Love to cook but don't have the time? Want to have more free time on a daily basis? Then this is your book. These are easy and affordable recipes, kid-tested and family-approved. Eat well and have more time—what a combination!"

—*Marriage Magazine*

"This book belongs in every family's kitchen! One of the best time- and money-savers a busy family can have."

—Gary Foreman, editor, *The Dollar Stretcher*

"There are shopping lists and recipes for two-week and 30-day meal plans. There's even a 10-day plan designed to eliminate cooking over the Christmas and New Year holidays. What a stress reliever!"

—*The Daily News*, Washington

"Finally a book that is so cooking-friendly ANYONE can follow the steps."

—Sherry Stacy, weekly radio host, *Recipes for Life* on KVSN

"Whether you cook for one month or one week, I am sure everyone can reap benefit from this book."

—Keith C. Heirdorn, publisher, *Living Gently Quarterly*

"*Frozen Assets* will be at the top of my recommended books list!"

—Rebecca Stuck, advice columnist, *Ask Miss Frugal*

"And she's done an impressive job with this book, which outlines step-by-step the shopping, cooking and freezing processes that have worked so well."

—*Copley News Service*

"Details a plan for cooking and freezing in quantity, with grocery lists, shopping lists, storage tips and dollar-stretching hints. The recipes are simple and straightforward, using everyday ingredients."

—*Atlanta Journal*

"A perfect gift for a busy homemaker."

—*The News-Herald Newspapers*

"Provides shopping lists and delicious recipes that will help you save time in the kitchen and money in the grocery store."

—*The Oak Ridger*, Tennessee

FROZEN ASSETS

DEBORAH TAYLOR-HOUGH

SOURCEBOOKS, INC.®
NAPERVILLE, ILLINOIS

Published by Sourcebooks, Inc.
P.O. Box 4410, Naperville, Illinois 60567-4410
(630) 961-3900
Fax: (630) 961-2168
www.sourcebooks.com

Originally published in 2002 by Champion Press, Ltd.

Library of Congress Cataloging-in-Publication Data

Taylor-Hough, Deborah.
  Frozen assets : cook for a day, eat for a month / by Deborah Taylor-Hough.
     p. cm.
  Includes index.
1. Cookery (Frozen foods) 2. Quick and easy cookery. I. Title.
  TX828.T3999 2009
  641.6'153--dc22
                              2009002537

Ingram
7/10   *14.99*   *42743*

Printed and bound in the United States of America.
VP 10 9 8 7 6 5 4 3 2 1

Also by Deborah Taylor-Hough

Frozen Assets Lite and Easy

Dedication

This book is dedicated to Stuart, Kelsey, Ian, and Shannon, who put up with endless new recipes and freezer experiments. You, my loving family, provided tireless support and encouragement, and you also allowed me the time to write, study, maintain Web pages, answer email, and cook.

Thank you!

CONTENTS

★ ★ ★

ACKNOWLEDGMENTS

My deepest appreciation to:

Dad—You gave me the computer, which ultimately led to writing this book. How can I thank you enough?

Brook N.—You believed in this project as much as I did. Thanks for your encouragement and editing.

Vicki M.—Thanks for suggesting a freezer-meal discussion and planting the seeds in my mind for this book.

Di J. and Chris S.—Your neighborliness (and the use of your large stock-pots!) made much of this possible.

Lisa M., Evelyn S., Karen S., Catherine L., and Barb M.—Your friendship, prayers, and faith in me never wavered.

Leon F.—You always had a moment to share your experience and practical knowledge with a new writer.

Steven G.—From your example, I learned to run an effective email discussion group.

Deb V., Gloriamarie A., Lynn N., and Sue (in Scotland)—Your cooking wisdom, recipes, advice, and humor never failed to inspire me.

And to all the other participants on the OAMC discussion group, thank you for sending your tips, questions, comments, recipes, encouragement, and most of all, your friendship—without all of you, this book never would've been written. I wish I could mention each of you by name, but there's not enough room on this page for the hundreds of personal acknowledgments it would require. (But I know who you are, and I appreciate every one of you!)

INTRODUCTION

I've been using bulk-cooking methods for five years. The book *Once-a-Month Cooking,* by Mimi Wilson and Mary Beth Lagerborg, revolutionized the way I feed my family. Although I found the recipes in *Once-a-Month Cooking* more expensive to prepare than my budget allowed, I adapted many of their techniques using my own recipes, and we've been saving money on groceries ever since. Also, not cooking a main dish from scratch every day allows me to save both time and effort. (My time is worth money, too!)

In February of 1997, an email discussion began between Vicki Madden and me on the subject of cooking for the freezer. Vicki had visited my frugal-living Web page and noticed that I enjoyed freezer-meal cooking. She had recently prepared a special Christmas gift for her boyfriend—a freezer full of frozen dinners. Vicki dropped me a note and asked if I'd like to share thoughts and experiences about freezer-meal cooking. Soon, we were exchanging tips, ideas, and favorite recipes. At the time, I was a stay-at-home mother of three, and Vicki was a single working mother of one; the input from our divergent lifestyles and family sizes made for a fun and stimulating conversation.

On a whim, I asked other online friends if they'd be interested in joining our once-a-month cooking (OAMC) discussion. I was surprised when nearly everyone I contacted replied, "Yes! I'd love to join a group like that!" Thus began an idea with a mind of its own. Our little two-person conversation grew to include hundreds of people from all walks of life, family backgrounds, economic levels, and geographic locations. I now maintain a popular OAMC Web page that averages 4,000-plus visitors each month—this is obviously an idea with wide appeal.

Many of the tips, recipes, and comments throughout this cookbook come from the international group of men and women who have participated in my online OAMC mailing list. I wrote this book in response to the demand I've received for an affordable and easy-to-follow book on freezer meals for people who are new to the concept.

My desire is that this book will help fill that need.

—Debi

1
★ ★ ★

THE ATTRACTION OF FROZEN ASSETS

Following the premature birth of our first child, a group of friends from church filled our freezer with more than two weeks' worth of frozen meals. Between frequent visits to the hospital nursery and the normal stresses of starting a new family, those meals in the freezer were a lifesaver.

During a later pregnancy, I wound up on bed rest for nearly four weeks. Once again, the ladies from church came to our aid with frozen dinners. One woman overwhelmed me when she showed up at my door laden with several shopping bags full of ready-to-cook frozen dinners—all from her personal stock of freezer meals.

The meals I received after my daughter's premature birth were my introduction to the concept of frozen meals. Since then, I've applied this method to our regular family menus and have saved substantial time, effort, and money in the process. Some cookbooks refer to this as investment cooking, once-a-month cooking, bulk cooking, or cooking ahead. I call my method "Frozen Assets," since dinner in the freezer can be like money in the bank.

Whether you're a stay-at-home mom creatively trying to make ends meet, a working parent searching for more hours in your hectic day, a single person looking for ideas for preparing home-cooked meals without leftovers, someone interested in the outreach opportunities frozen meals can provide, or anyone who needs to save money or find a few more hours in their day, *Frozen Assets* could be your answer.

The people I've met who are actively involved with freezer-meal cooking methods represent a large and growing cross section of the population: single, married, stay-at-home parents, part-time workers, full-time working parents, working couples with no children, business owners, big happy families, and small happy families. And they're living all over the world—throughout the United States, Canada, the United Kingdom, New Zealand, Australia, and elsewhere.

Freezer-meal cooks are also active in a variety of personal pursuits that put frequent demands on their time and financial resources: pursuing full-time careers; consulting work; freelance writing; performing research on genealogy; volunteering; organizing PTA groups; transporting children to various functions; coaching or participating in sports; homeschooling; Sunday-school teaching; and leading and attending various types of study groups, co-ops, military functions, church activities, community events, piano recitals, music ministry, knitting, adult-education programs, college studies, and more.

People from all walks of life are reaping the benefits of this simple, common-sense approach to cooking and meal planning. In a recent survey, I asked the question, "What first attracted you to make-ahead cooking?" The answers I received from the survey participants were varied. Maybe you can relate to some of the following statements:

"I hate coming home and trying to figure out what to have for dinner, especially because I don't enjoy cooking. I can put up with it for one day—if it means I don't have to cook for the rest of the month."

"I was attracted by the idea of saving money—not having to buy fast food because I'm too busy to think about cooking every night, even though I love to cook."

"Trying to make ends meet with this tribe is a constant challenge, and I can use all the help I can get!"

"I like the idea of the organization presented in OAMC. It seems that it would help out the budget as well."

"I am diabetic. I also love to eat out because I'm often too tired to cook. I thought if I already had healthy food prepared, I'd be more apt to stick to my diabetic routine and not spend so much money at restaurants."

"My mother recently passed away, and I'm worried about my dad not eating properly. I'm going to freeze single servings of our regular family meals to put in Dad's freezer. That way, I can be assured he's eating a hot, home-cooked meal each evening instead of just another TV dinner."

"I'm currently trying to cut corners wherever possible in order to get our financial house in order—cooking for the freezer sounds like it's definitely a time saver and a money saver."

"I like being organized, so I like to have meals in the freezer or a supper ready in the fridge for the next night we're busy."

"As a homeschooler, I have a lot more flexibility in what we can do. If we spend all day at a museum or park, all we have to do is pop dinner in the oven when we get home. It really cuts down on those grab-a-burger-on-the-way-home meals."

"We only get paid once a month. It would help our budgeting."

"Bulk buying and bulk cooking—I love it!"

"I love not having to think about what to fix for dinner each night—5:00 p.m. is a stressful time at my house—hubby is just wrapping up work and my daughter wants attention. Now I can relax and enjoy my family."

"I read that cooking for the freezer would save time and money, and enable me to have meals available if someone had a need in their family (sickness, new baby, etc.)."

"I'm single and practice a modified version of cooking once for a month. I started this when I was commuting by train—a three-hour round trip plus a very stressful eight-hour day. When I arrived home it was usually bread and cheese and fall into bed, so I developed a routine of cooking ahead for the freezer."

"Invariably, I would stand at the refrigerator every night at 5:00 p.m. wondering, 'What am I going to fix?' After twelve to fifteen hours at work each day, I didn't want to even think about cooking. I also wanted to save money by not eating out as often."

"The time and money savings, as well as the added convenience of not worrying about what the kids were going to eat when I was at work, attracted me to freezer meals."

Although the reasons for bulk cooking are varied, the basic premise remains the same—saving time, effort, and money by creating a stock of homemade meals in your freezer for later use.

You may choose to cook all day and stock up a month's worth of meals in your freezer (or two months of meals—or more!). You might spread your bulk cooking out over the course of several days. You may decide to cook freezer meals periodically, taking advantage of sales at the market. You might like doubling or tripling recipes as you cook during the week—adding the extra batches to your stash of Frozen Assets.

Whichever method of cooking for the freezer you choose, I believe you'll find *Frozen Assets* to be a wise, money-saving, and time-saving investment in your family's health, peace of mind, and financial well being.

2
★ ★ ★

"HELP! MY FREEZER IS TOO SMALL," AND OTHER FREQUENTLY ASKED QUESTIONS

The following are questions people frequently ask about frozen meals and make-ahead cooking.

"I only have the small freezer above my refrigerator. Can I still do a full month's worth of cooking ahead?"

You might want to consider twice-a-month cooking at first, just until you get used to the method and used to packing your freezer tightly. Eventually, you may be able to store an entire month's worth of entrées in your fridge-top freezer with careful planning. Use heavy-duty freezer bags to freeze food more compactly than in casserole dishes or foil pans. Freeze the bags flat, and stack them carefully. Clear out nonessentials from the freezer before cooking day. Wait until the freezer clears out later in the month before stocking up on frozen bread, ice cream, etc. To save space, prepare meals with sauces to pour over noodles or rice, but don't freeze the noodles or rice ahead; cook them up fresh when you serve the sauce.

"I don't have much money to buy a new freezer, but I would like to purchase a separate freezer. Where should I go to find one?"

Ask friends, relatives, and neighbors to keep an eye out for people who are moving out of state or updating their kitchen. I've known several people who have gotten freezers for free just by making a few phone calls. Check the newspaper. Look at garage sales, yard sales, and appliance repair stores. Try auctions of dented white goods.

"How do you keep track of which meals are in the freezer and which have been used?"

Post a list of all meals on your freezer door, either on paper or a small white board. Mark the meals off the list as you use them.

"How do I cook for an entire day with two toddlers underfoot?"

Some possibilities: Cook with a friend and then trade off childcare and cooking duty; have a spouse or relative take the children out for the day; enlist a friend or neighbor to watch your kids that day and offer to watch hers in return; let the kids spend the day with their grandparents; or barter some frozen home-cooked meals in exchange for a few hours of baby-sitting.

"How do I know what will freeze well and what won't?"

If you're unsure, freeze a small amount as a test. For a listing of foods that don't freeze well or that change in the freezing process, see Appendix A.

"What can I use for freezer containers?"

Plastic food storage boxes and metal, glass, and ceramic bakeware work well. Be sure to check garage sales and thrift stores for these items. Freezer bags also work well. Use heavy-duty bags specifically intended for freezer usage; do not use regular food storage bags.

If you prepare and store freezer meals in rectangular shapes, you may actually get more into your freezer than before since you won't have lumpy packages and round containers taking up excess room.

Almost any plastic food-grade container is safe for freezing food, but don't use plastic containers in the microwave unless they say they're safe for that purpose. Plastics not specifically made for heating can release harmful chemicals into your food.

You can also line baking pans with heavy-duty aluminum foil. Add your meal, cook if necessary, and let cool. Put the baking pan filled with the meal into the freezer. When the meal is frozen solid, remove the frozen meal and foil from the baking dish, wrap the meal completely with more foil, label it, and freeze it. To reheat, simply place the frozen foil-wrapped meal back into the original pan you used for freezing.

"If I do the complete thirty–day meal cooking, will it be a huge initial investment to buy a full month's worth of food?"

It depends on how elaborate your meals are, and how much you cook from scratch. Convenience foods are much more expensive than their homemade counterparts. It might cost a bit more the first time, but because you'll be purchasing some items in bulk, the cost could actually be quite a bit less than you would expect. Recipes that use a lot of premade items can be expensive to prepare. Chapter Ten contains a collection of money-saving ideas for grocery shopping.

"My kitchen is tiny. How can I handle a large amount of cooking in such a small space?"

Make extra counter space by turning off the gas stove and lighting burners as needed. Set up a card table in the living room. Use the kitchen or dining room table for food prep. If the washer and dryer are near the kitchen, use these for additional countertops. Organize yourself by thinking through your cooking steps ahead of time.

"How do I label things? What sort of labels, pens, etc., do I need? What should I write on the labels?"

Inexpensive freezer labels applied to the foil before freezing will usually work fine. If you use freezer paper, you can write directly on it with a grease pencil. You can use a Sharpie brand permanent marker to write directly on the foil or freezer bag. A wet-erase marker also works well on foil. Avoid masking tape, since it won't stick at low temperatures. Another labeling suggestion is to double-bag meals in freezer bags and slip an index card with the labeling information between the two bags. On your label, write the name of the meal, the date it was frozen, the number of servings, the reheating directions, and any other special instructions (i.e. sprinkle with 1 cup grated cheese before baking, etc.).

"I love this idea of cooking for my freezer, but I don't have a full day available for cooking. Are there other ways of cooking ahead?"

You can cook three or four meals at a time rather than a whole month's worth. Or spread out your cooking by preparing all of your chicken recipes one day, ground beef recipes another, spaghetti-sauce recipes on a third day, and then vegetarian or cooked bean recipes on a fourth day.

Doubling and tripling recipes will also help you quickly build up a stock of frozen meals. It really doesn't take more time to make a large pot of spaghetti for freezing extras than it does to make a single meal's worth of sauce.

"Are all the freezer meals casseroles and pasta-with-sauce dishes?"

You can freeze almost anything: soups, casseroles, sandwiches, meals to serve over rice, chicken dishes, etc.

"I'm a vegetarian. Any special tips?"

There shouldn't be any problem with adapting this method to vegetarian menus. When you prepare your regular recipes, try freezing a single portion before you attempt a large batch of freezer meals. (This tip also applies to any recipe you haven't tried in the freezer.) Tofu, TVP (texturized vegetable protein), and cooked dry beans all freeze well.

"Are there special pots, pans, utensils, or appliances I should consider having on hand to make the big cooking day go easier?"

★ A food processor for chopping large quantities of onions, celery, etc.

★ A set of high-quality, sharp knives.

★ Several large stockpots (the heavier, the better).

★ Long-handled spoons, for stirring and mixing.

★ A good can opener—an electric one isn't necessary, but it will make the process easier.

★ Crockpots, for slow cooking.

★ A salad-shooter type of appliance, for grating large amounts of cheese.

★ An automatic bag-sealing machine for sucking the air out of bags and sealing them for the freezer. These can often be found inexpensively at garage sales.

★ Buy or borrow a waffle iron to make homemade frozen waffles if you are cooking breakfast items ahead; homemade waffles are much tastier than the ones bought from the grocery freezer case.

Note: You don't necessarily have to run out and purchase all of these items right away. I often borrow a neighbor's large stockpot and waffle iron on my cooking days.

3
★ ★ ★

A DAY IN THE LIFE OF FROZEN ASSETS

The following is a description of a bulk-cooking session at my house. Many people have told me it proved helpful to them as they planned their first round of freezer meals.

Thursday—Early Evening

I've stared at my empty freezer long enough.

Tonight, I'll sit down, plan my month's menus, and make out a shopping list for tomorrow morning. Saturday will be cooking day. It takes me about six hours of one day to complete a full month of cooking main dinner meals. That's a long day of cooking, true, but having a home-cooked meal available every day for a month with no more fuss than just the preparation of a side dish and salad is heaven! One of the best parts of cooking ahead is taking those armloads of yummy dinners out to the freezer.

My husband's work schedule is one of the main reasons I tried once-a-month cooking in the first place. I knew I needed to do something differently to work around our unusual family schedule. My husband often works odd shifts, so we frequently need to eat our main meal at noon during the week.

If I don't have dinner in the freezer, I end up spending much of the morning (our family time) preparing our noon meal—or we run out to the local taco stand for $0.59 tacos.

A friend suggested cooking for the freezer so I wouldn't have to take up our only time together as a family with cooking and meal preparation. My initial response was, "I'd love to try that, but we don't have a separate freezer—just the little one over the refrigerator. I don't have enough room to store a month's worth of meals."

My friend encouraged me to start small, doing twice-a-month cooking and packing the meals in freezer bags for more compact stacking in the freezer. It sounded reasonable. I rolled up my sleeves and gave twice-a-month cooking a try. Those two weeks of frozen meals were wonderful.

Eventually, I learned that, by using freezer bags, I could pack an entire month's worth of meals in our little fridge-top freezer. The first two weeks of the month, we didn't have room for frozen bread or ice cream, but having those prepared meals was definitely more important to my sanity than stocking up on bread and eating frozen desserts the entire month.

Recently, my father purchased a larger freezer for himself and gave his small chest freezer to us. (Thanks, Dad!) Now I don't have to freeze every dinner in a freezer bag, and we can stock up on bread from the bakery thrift stores again. With the separate freezer, I even find ice cream in the house now and then.

I want to encourage those of you who are thinking, "Someday, I'll try once-a-month cooking—*after* I get a bigger freezer." Give it a go right now, even though you don't have a big freezer. Try twice-a-month cooking stored in freezer bags to start.

I've discovered that buying in bulk for these big cooking days can easily save enough money to pay for a good used freezer. Check your newspaper ads. You never know what kind of deals you might come across. Ask friends, relatives, and neighbors to let you know if they hear of anyone moving out of state or remodeling their kitchen. I've known several families who have gotten freezers for free just by making a few phone calls. You never know what you might come across when you start asking around.

I need to sit down with my paper, pen, and favorite cookbooks. Planning night tonight…for tomorrow I shop!

Thursday Night—Later

The first part of my OAMC is done—menu planning. This is what I'm going to make:

Sloppy Joes (three meals)

Broccoli Quiche (three meals)

Spaghetti (three meals)

Chicken Creole (three meals)

French Bread Pizza (two meals)

Enchiladas (five meals)

Cabbage Casserole (five meals)

Veggie-Fish Dinner (four meals)

Broccoli Chicken (four meals)

Baked Macaroni Casserole (four meals)

Scalloped Potatoes with Ham (five meals)

That list means forty-one meals will be stacked in my freezer by Saturday night. There will also be at least four meals of homemade vegetable chicken soup made from leftovers thrown into the chicken stock.

My personal freezer meals cookbook is a simple three-ring binder. I've filled it with plastic page protectors that I slip recipes into, plus shopping lists and other freezer meal-related information. I'm always updating my notebook as I find new recipes and tips.

I have several meal plans that I often follow, but I adapt the plan to what I have on hand, or any specific requests that my family makes. A while ago, I set up master shopping lists for my favorite meal plans. I ran off a supply of photocopies, and I keep the shopping lists in the opening pages of my notebook. When it's time to plan my menu and go shopping, I can slip one of the master shopping lists out of its page protector, and I'm ready to add to the list as needed. This saves having to rethink my entire shopping list each time.

The next page in my notebook is a list called "Order of Preparation of Thirty Meals." I have everything pretty well laid out: what I need to cook the night before; what I need to do first; what order to prepare the meals; etc. I have the recipes I use most frequently in the next section of my notebook. I have a separate section for other recipes that have already been adapted to my way of freezer-meal cooking, and then another section of frequently used recipes my family loves. My goal is to incorporate more of those recipes into my OAMC plans.

Eventually, I hope to have six different master lists, so I will only have to repeat the same monthly plan twice a year.

Tomorrow, I shop. I'll let you have a look at my shopping list and the final bill after I'm done.

Friday Afternoon

My shopping trip took just over one hour—about seventy minutes, including check-out time. I do all my grocery shopping at one store, since I'm always strapped for time when I shop. Since our family has only one car, my time at the store is limited. I could probably save more money if I shopped around for better prices at different stores, but my time and effort is worth money, too. The store I've chosen for my regular shopping is the one I've found to be generally cheaper all around than the other stores in town.

To purchase ingredients for forty-plus main-dish meals to feed our family of five (plus salad fixings, fruits, vegetables, shampoo, dish soap, paper products, milk, eggs, cereal, peanut butter, jelly, bread, etc.), I spent $200 grocery shopping on Friday. I had taken $225 with me to the store, so after everything was said and done, I had enough money left to buy myself an espresso and a U-Bake Pizza (large pepperoni, for $7.50) for our dinner on shopping day. Nice treat.

People have asked what exactly I was able to purchase for so little money. I already had on hand some of the items on my master shopping list, but I also needed to stock up on a few things I normally have around—so I guess it all balances out.

Several weeks before, one of our local grocery stores had a sale on ground beef (10-pound packages for $0.99 per pound), so I had already purchased my ground beef, divided it into 1-pound packages, and put them into the freezer. We also had enough ham in the freezer for the Scalloped Potatoes with Ham recipe. To save money, I almost always purchase turkey ham—especially if it's going to be added into a recipe and not eaten alone. Someone had given me twelve 1-pound cans of tomato sauce, so I didn't need to buy that item, either. I also had quite a bit of frozen and canned vegetables around, so I didn't need to purchase any additional vegetables for side dishes. I'll have to restock in two weeks when my husband gets paid again, though.

If I had purchased the above-mentioned items, it would've added $10 for the ground beef, $3 for the turkey ham, $2 for the tomato sauce, and about $5 for the frozen vegetables. If I add that to the $200 I spent on Friday, my total bill would've been about $220.

Here's what I purchased:

2 pounds of white fish (whatever was on sale)

2 whole chickens

2 pounds of bulk Italian sausage

2 packages hot dogs

2 taco seasoning packets

10 pounds of onions

3 large heads of cabbage

2 pounds of carrots

4 pounds of broccoli

1 bunch celery

2 large green peppers

10 pounds of potatoes

2 heads of lettuce

10 pounds of oranges

5 pounds of bananas

2 small cans of tomato paste

4 cans of Italian stewed tomatoes

1 can of green chiles

1 large can of sliced black olives

4 jars of good-quality spaghetti sauce

Soda crackers

2 cans of enchilada sauce

1 box of licorice spice tea

Cornmeal

Biscuit mix

Liquid foundation (make-up)

4 pounds of Cheddar cheese

1 pound of mozzarella cheese

3 gallons of 2% milk

1 large carton of fat-free sour cream

18 eggs

Paper napkins

Ream of computer paper

Toilet paper

Paper towels

1 package of 30 corn tortillas

5 pounds of dried spaghetti

2 pounds of macaroni noodles

1½ cups millet

Large bag of Asian rice

Olive oil

1 pound of margarine

Large bottle of lemon juice

4 loaves of sandwich bread

1 loaf of French bread (for French Bread Pizza)

3 packs of hamburger buns

2 packs of hot dog buns

12 (8-inch) square foil pans

Dish soap

Kitty litter

Cat food

1 gallon of vinegar

Large bottle of ketchup

Mustard

Worcestershire sauce

Peanut butter

Jelly

2 packages of store-brand allergy medicine

Aluminum foil

Breakfast cereal

When the cashier bagged up my groceries, there were fourteen full shopping bags. I frequently hear amazed comments from cashiers about how little my groceries cost. They tell me when they see that amount of groceries, it's usually well over $300—if not closer to $350. There's no great secret to shopping carefully. A penny saved here and there can add up quickly when purchasing large amounts of food. (I've included a list of money-saving tips for grocery shopping in Chapter Ten.)

I usually purchase store brands unless I know for certain that my family doesn't like them. For example, I've tried making my spaghetti sauce with jars of generic sauce. That got a big thumbs-down from everyone. Now, I purchase good-quality name-brand sauce, or I make my own. Usually one of the big name brands is on sale, so I purchase the sale brand. My family can really tell the difference between cheap spaghetti sauce and the better brands. With other items, they're not quite so picky. I try generic items or store brands, and if they don't go over well, I don't use them again.

Sunday Afternoon

Thursday night, I did my menu planning. Friday, I shopped. Saturday, I cooked. By Sunday morning, I had more than forty meals in my freezer. Phew…what a relief to be done with it for another month.

We are a family of five: Dad, Mom, an eleven-year-old girl, an eight-year-old boy, and a three-year-old girl. My husband is one of those people who can eat twice as much as any other person on the planet and never gain a pound. I am not like that, by the way. I can gain weight by just looking at pictures of food in magazines. My son can eat four full bowls of breakfast cereal in the morning and still be hungry.

On Friday night, I cooked the chicken in a large stockpot and put it in the refrigerator to cool overnight. I also made spaghetti sauce on Friday since it goes together so quickly; I ended up with enough for four meals of spaghetti and two for pizza. I browned the ground beef and chopped the vegetables: onions, pepper, celery, and carrots.

This was my order of preparation on cooking day, more or less:

1. Bone and chop the chicken. Put stock in the refrigerator.

2. Cook rice.

3. Cut ham into ½-inch cubes.

4. Cook and slice potatoes.

5. Prepare meals.

6. Use leftover vegetables, meats, tomato sauce, noodles, and whatever else to make soup with the broth from cooking the chicken.

The total time spent cooking on Friday night and Saturday was about seven hours, including a break for lunch and a visit from extended family members in the afternoon. The relatives who stopped by didn't know I cooked bulk freezer meals, so they were curious about what I was doing. It became educating-the-relatives day at my house. One of them stayed in the kitchen with me for about twenty minutes, watching me cook and asking questions. He's fascinated by how things work and how certain activities create efficiencies, increase productivity, and that sort of thing. I think my explanations passed muster.

I realized after I was finished cooking on Saturday that an added benefit of cooking ahead is that I have more desire to prepare other things during the week when I'm not so focused on getting a main course prepared each day. When I know I only have to warm something up, I tend to do extra baking and special cooking. I enjoy cooking, but the daily-ness of it wears thin after awhile. For me, Frozen Assets restores the joy of cooking special things. Tomorrow, I'm going to fix a batch of my Million-Dollar Chocolate Chip Cookies and some homemade cornbread to go with our freezer meal of enchiladas.

And that's the end of my description of a day in the life of cooking ahead at my house. I hope it was helpful and gave you some food for thought. (Pardon the pun!)

THE INS AND OUTS OF
MEAL PLANNING

Although the practice of preparing an entire month's worth of meals in one day is popular right now, there are other methods of cooking ahead that may be more user-friendly, especially for people new to the idea. I recommend starting with small, manageable steps. If the idea of once-a-month cooking is intimidating, try twice-a-month or once-a-week cooking. Same methods, but less work at one time.

Another easy and painless way to start building up a supply of Frozen Assets is by doubling or tripling recipes as you prepare them during the week. If you're making a casserole for tonight's dinner, prepare three instead. This way, you can eat one and freeze the other two for later meals. Tripling recipes for one week will give you a two-week stock of frozen meals with very little extra effort. When you prepare a double or triple batch (one to eat and the others to freeze), set the freezer batches aside a few minutes before they're fully cooked. Slightly undercooking meats, pastas, and vegetables prevents overcooking and that warmed-over flavor you sometimes get when reheating after freezing.

Cooking a large pot of spaghetti sauce can help establish your Frozen Assets.

The last time I made spaghetti sauce, I added to my freezer three meals of lasagna, two meals of pizza, and four meals of sauce to serve over pasta. Nine meals from one easy cooking session—not a bad return on my investment.

Often, ground beef or turkey will go on sale for a great price if purchased in bulk. I stock up on sale-priced meats, cook the meals ahead, and add to my Frozen Assets.

Meatballs prepared ahead can be served in a variety of ways: in home-made vegetable or minestrone soup, with condensed mushroom soup and sour cream to create a stroganoff served over rice or noodles, with brown gravy and potatoes or rice, and with barbecue or spaghetti sauce served in small French rolls for sandwiches. Meatloaf freezes well, and its leftovers make wonderful hot or cold sandwiches.

Andrea, the mother of a two-year-old and six months pregnant with twins, is starting her cooking now for those busy post-partum days. Realizing her hands will soon be full (literally!), she says, "I don't have the stamina to de-vote an entire day to standing on my feet cooking, unless I want to send my-self into labor right now! I'm going to triple recipes of easy meals every night until the babies come. I know the extra work now will pay off big when I find myself less crazy over meal preparation as I'm caring for our new little ones."

Recently divorced or widowed individuals often find themselves over-whelmed with the idea of cooking every meal for just one person. It's an in-credibly stressful time of life, and people need to guard their health by eating regular, healthy meals. Many people facing sudden singleness end up fre-quenting the local drive-through restaurants or stocking up on TV dinners. It's easier and healthier just to reach into the freezer each day and pull out a home-cooked meal that's ready to heat and serve.

Adapting these methods for singles is a common dilemma facing many cooks who are considering cooking ahead. I've prepared a list of sugges-tions in Appendix C for the single person desiring the convenience of freezer meals.

Getting Started with Ease

If you're new to freezer-meal cooking, I recommend starting with one of this book's suggested meal plans. This way, you won't have to focus on developing a plan from scratch—just follow the simple steps that are provided. After completing this routine a couple of times, you'll begin to sense the patterns, which will make adapting your own recipes much easier. Read through the planning section of this book to get a feel for what you'll be doing, but don't worry about remembering every detail. The menu plans will guide you step-by-step through the entire process.

Menu Choice and Planning for the Trailblazers

So you want to start right in with your own family recipes and make your own meal plan? Great! First, we need to do a little planning. To begin, figure out how often you and your family are willing to eat the same meal in a single month. Some people refuse to eat the same meal more than once during a four-week period; others don't mind eating the same meal as often as four or five times a month—provided it's not four days in a row. If you decide to eat each meal twice during the month, you will need to choose fifteen recipes. I usually choose ten recipes and triple them for a month's worth of meals. Many of the recipes in this book have already been doubled or tripled for your convenience.

When preparing your meal plan, choose foods you're certain your family will enjoy. There are few things worse for a freezer-meal cook than a freezer filled with food no one will eat. The recipes you choose for a thirty-day cooking experience should be simple. An experienced freezer-meal cook told me, "If you can't visualize the steps in your mind, it's too complicated!"

Try to choose a variety of main dishes. For example, choose several from each category: poultry, ground beef, pork, seafood, cheese, pasta, and beans.

I base my monthly plan on what's currently stored in my cupboards or freezer. I also take into account the sales at the local market.

The following types of dishes work especially well for the freezer: sauces (tomato, meat, and gravy), main dishes, casseroles, stews, soups, meat pies, meat dishes in gravy (Swiss steak or meatballs), cooked poultry, roasts, chops, burgers, tofu, TVP, sandwiches (omit jelly, mayonnaise, and lettuce), shellfish, most baked goods (cookies, breads, and cakes), goulashes, meatloaf, and cooked dried beans.

The following types of items don't work well in the freezer: egg-based sauces, milk or cream-based sauces, salads, stuffed poultry, dishes with bread crumbs or dry toppings (add toppings after freezing and before reheating), fish steaks and fillets, and baked fruit pies (they turn out soggy). See Appendix A for a more complete list of foods that are unsuitable for the freezer.

I recommend implementing your cooking plan over the course of three days. I like to plan one day. In the evening of day two, I usually do my shopping and prepare as much as I can ahead of time. On day three, I do the actual meal assembly, which takes about six to seven hours.

Making a List and Checking It Twice (Shopping)

To simplify meal planning for the month, I take out a blank calendar page and fill in all the meals that I plan to prepare on the calendar. Writing the meals down helps to prevent accidentally serving several ground beef meals in a row, or winding up with three meals of spaghetti sauce for the last week of the month. I've often used a blank magnetic wipe-off calendar on my refrigerator, but a regular calendar page or daily planner works just as well.

The day before you shop, take a look at the recipes you've chosen. Write down every ingredient (and their exact amounts) on a sheet of paper. Then, go through your cupboards and refrigerator, crossing off everything you already have on hand. Check amounts carefully. If you need three 16-ounce jars of tomato sauce (48 ounces total), make sure you actually have the correct amount in ounces on hand before crossing that item off your list. After you complete the inventory of your cupboards, the remaining ingredients will be your shopping list.

Next, figure out what sort of containers you'll be using for freezing. If you need to purchase freezer bags, plastic wrap, foil, or aluminum trays, add these items to your shopping list. Organizing your shopping list according to categories—that is, meat, dairy, produce, canned goods, etc.—makes shopping easier and faster. I know the layout of my grocery store, so I organize my list according to store aisles.

Some shopping tips:

★ Don't shop when you're hungry. You might get tired and weak if you're hungry during a huge shopping trip, and you'll be more susceptible to impulse buys if you're hungry in the store.

★ Buy in bulk, when possible. If your recipes need three 8-ounce cans of tomato paste, look for one 24-ounce can. The cost per ounce will usually be significantly less in a larger package.

★ Contact the manufacturer directly if you're doing a lot of bulk buying to save even more money. A warehouse club may offer significant savings as well.

★ Familiarize yourself with common can sizes. Some cans look similar in size, but hold different amounts.

★ Look on the lowest and highest shelves for potential bargains. Stores often place the most expensive items at eye level.

★ Compare the cost of various forms of food—fresh, frozen, canned, and dried—using cost per serving.

★ Try generic or store brands. If they meet your quality needs and are okay with your family's individual tastes, you can save money by using private-brand labels.

★ Choose the grade and quality of meats or produce that best fits your intended use. Use the most inexpensive form when shape, uniformity of size, and color are not important.

★ Remember that you pay for fancy labels or extra packaging. Choose foods that are packaged simply.

★ Avoid convenience foods if you're trying to save money. Home-made alternatives are usually less expensive.

★ Leave your children at home when doing your major grocery shopping so you can concentrate on prices and finish your shopping as quickly as possible.

After you've arrived home from shopping, put away all perishable foods in your refrigerator and leave out canned goods and other items needed for cooking the next day. This will save you the hassle of putting everything away, only to take it all out again the next morning. Every little bit of time and effort you can save when bulk cooking will be appreciated.

Steps for a Successful Cooking Experience

Your first experience with a big cooking day will probably be the most difficult and longest, but you'll learn shortcuts and personal preferences as you go along. Each subsequent bulk-cooking day will get easier. After the big cooking day is done, you might ask yourself, "What did I do that for?" But after about two days of eating ready-made yummy meals, you'll forget all the labor that went into that freezer full of food.

Sort Your Recipes

Separate your recipes according to their main protein source: chicken, ground beef, dried beans, ham, and others. Plan on preparing the recipes in groups according to main ingredients. Read through your recipes, and break them down into steps. Plan to do similar steps together. If you'll need to brown ground beef for tacos, spaghetti sauce, and Sloppy Joes, brown all the meat together, maybe the night before, and then divide the browned meat when preparing the recipes.

Post Your Recipes for Easy Visibility

I keep my tried-and-true freezer recipes in plastic page protectors organized by main protein type in a three-ring binder. This way I can actually take the pages out of my notebook while I'm cooking and lay them on the table, tape them to the wall, or hang them with magnets on the refrigerator door.

Prepare Ahead

Prepare things ahead as much as possible. Decide which items to prepare the evening before, such as chopping vegetables, grating cheese, preparing spaghetti sauce, boiling chicken, or browning ground beef. It's easier to add chopped onions or grated cheese to your recipes if they're already prepared. A food processor is helpful at this stage of meal preparation. The evening before the big cooking day, I usually brown ground beef, boil chickens, prepare spaghetti sauce, chop vegetables, and grate cheese. Restaurants usually hire someone just to do the advance preparation, making the cooking process easier for the cooks. You might want to consider "hiring" your older children as your "prep cooks."

Preparing Chicken for Recipes

If you cook the chicken the night before, you can simply add the chicken as needed to your recipes on cooking day. To prepare, boil chicken(s) in a large Dutch oven or stockpot with enough water to fully cover it. Add several stalks of celery and some sliced onion. Boil until the meat is white to the bone and falls off the bone easily. After the chicken is cooked, cool it slightly, and place the pot in the refrigerator to cool completely overnight. The fat will congeal on top of the liquid, so you can easily scoop it away in the morning. Then, you can remove the chicken and bone it. Cut the meat into bite-sized portions and place them into a large bowl. Save the stock from the cooked chicken for making soup at the end of the day.

Get Ready, Get Set!

Before you begin your big day of cooking, assemble all necessary utensils, pots, pans, measuring cups, appliances, etc. You don't want to be scrambling around your kitchen looking for measuring spoons in the midst of a month's worth of cooking.

Sink o' Soap

While cooking, keep the sink filled with warm, soapy water. This way you can wash pots, pans, measuring cups, spoons, and other cooking utensils as you go. If you keep ahead of messes as you progress through the day, the cleanup won't become overwhelming.

If you don't usually wear an apron while cooking, this would be a good time to start. You also might choose to wear older clothes so your good clothes won't wind up with spills or food stains. Always keep your hands, equipment, and work areas clean to prevent contamination. Wash hands frequently, especially after handling raw meats. Tie back long hair.

Go For It! Three Easy Tips

TIP ONE: Chop vegetables and grate cheese first thing on cooking day if you didn't do it the day before.

TIP TWO: Prepare your most complicated recipes early in the day, while you're still fresh.

TIP THREE: Pack foods in quantities that will be used for a single family-sized meal.

Keeping the "Fresh" in Your "Frozen"

To prevent overcooking, or that warmed-over taste, slightly undercook foods that will be reheated after freezing. Cook vegetables and meats until just tender, not soft. Undercook pasta and rice; for best results, use converted rice.

When Your Stamina Is Simmering

Physical exhaustion is a common complaint after a full day of cooking. These tips should help cut down on some of the fatigue:

★ Wear supportive walking shoes. This isn't the day to cook in bare feet or bedroom slippers.

★ Wear comfortable clothes.

★ Go to bed early the night before.

★ Eat a good breakfast.

★ Remember to stop for lunch, and sit down while you eat.

★ Take frequent mini-breaks.

★ Do as much meal preparation as possible while sitting at the kitchen table.

★ Pull up a stool next to the counter and sit whenever you can.

★ Plan a special treat to look forward to afterward: go out to dinner; go on a picnic; take a long, relaxing bath; watch a favorite movie; or go to bed early.

★ Tell your spouse you'll make several of his or her favorite meals in exchange for a back rub or foot massage at the end of the day.

Freezing

If possible, reduce your freezer's temperature by 10 degrees for twenty-four hours before your big cooking day. Foods should be frozen at 0 degrees Fahrenheit or below to prevent spoilage and minimize changes in flavor, texture, and nutrients. Set your freezer to –10 degrees Fahrenheit before you start adding large amounts of unfrozen food to your freezer. After the food is frozen solid, return the temperature back to 0 degrees.

Label all freezer bags and containers with the name of the meal, the date it was frozen, the number of servings, heating instructions, and any other special preparation instructions, such as "sprinkle with 1 cup grated cheese before baking." Many frozen foods look alike after freezing, so don't skip the labeling step. Trust me—you don't want to play "Guess-the-Frozen-Meal" when you're looking for tomorrow's dinner.

Cool food quickly before placing it in the freezer. Don't let food stand at room temperature for longer than thirty minutes. Either set the meal in the refrigerator in a shallow container or place it into a shallow pan in a sink partially filled with ice water. Stir the food frequently during the cooling process. To prevent large ice crystals from forming as your meal freezes, food should be no warmer than room temperature when you place it into the freezer.

Use good quality, durable, leak-proof, and moisture-proof freezer bags, foils, and plastic containers. This isn't the time to scrimp on packaging. Make sure any plastic containers you use for freezing are food-grade plastic. Also, if the labels on packaging material don't indicate that the material is made for use in the freezer, it probably isn't. It's no bargain to recycle plastic vegetable or bread bags if your food and hard work leaks out of them.

Remove air from your freezer bags either by pressing the air out with your hands, starting at the bottom and working up toward the opening, or by using a drinking straw to suck out the excess air before sealing the bag. Removing excess air will prevent freezer burn while also making flatter bags in order to maximize freezer space. Pack freezer containers tightly, without air pockets, but remember to leave a head space of at least 1-inch to allow liquid-based meals to expand during freezing.

Conserve freezer space by freezing bags flat and then stacking them on end. Some cooks freeze large liquid-filled bags inside empty cardboard cereal boxes. When the boxes are removed, you'll have easy-to-stack bricks of frozen food.

Prepared meals can be frozen directly in your casserole or baking dishes. If you'll be reheating in the same container, be aware that glass dishes can break if put directly into a preheated oven unless the manufacturer specifies the container is safe from freezer to oven. Casserole dishes can be freed for other uses by lining them with heavy-duty aluminum foil before filling. After the meal has been baked and frozen, remove it from the dish, wrap it fully, then seal, label, and store it in the freezer.

When you are ready to reheat, you can save time by packaging foods in freezer-to-microwave-safe containers.

Tomato-based items and other acidic foods will react with aluminum, eating holes through your foil or aluminum baking pans. Oiling or coating the pans and foil with nonstick cooking spray helps to prevent this problem.

Thawing, Serving, and Dealing with Power Outages

Most main dishes can be reheated either with or without thawing first. If you want to completely thaw the meal first, take the frozen dinner out of your freezer thirty-six to forty-eight hours before you need to use it. This assures that it won't still be frozen when mealtime arrives. Thaw meals in your refrigerator rather than on the countertop to avoid spoilage. You can thaw frozen food packed in a plastic freezer bag by immersing the bag in a bowl or sink of cold water. Change the water frequently.

For heating frozen precooked meals, use the temperature setting originally used for cooking the meal. Then, cook the meal for slightly less than double the original cooking time. For example, if a casserole originally baked for thirty minutes, start with reheating the fully frozen meal for fifty minutes, checking carefully near the end of the cooking time to prevent overcooking. Casseroles are done when the edges are bubbly and the center is hot.

Microwave ovens do an excellent job of reheating. Check your manufacturer's directions for specific instructions and times.

For quick reheating of frozen sauces or creamy foods, use a double boiler. Start with warm, not hot, water in the bottom section; this prevents food from sticking and becoming mushy. Partial thawing in the refrigerator will speed up the heating process.

To avoid moisture buildup, thaw breaded foods in the refrigerator overnight with the freezer bag opened or removed.

Most baked goods, such as breads, rolls, muffins, and cakes, can be thawed quickly and safely at room temperature. Exceptions include fruit pies and any items with cream-based or watery fillings. Keep baked goods wrapped in their original packing to prevent dryness and condensation.

If you suffer a power outage, keep your freezer closed. Little or no thawing should occur within the first twelve to twenty hours. If your freezer is full of food and the power will be out longer than one day, you have two options. You can either move the contents of your freezer to a rental frozen food locker, or you can purchase dry ice for your freezer. If you use dry ice, lay cardboard over the packages in your freezer and place dry ice on the cardboard. Never place dry ice directly onto your packages of food, and always wear heavy gloves when handling dry ice. A 50-pound block of dry ice should keep your food frozen for two to three days.

Twelve Additional Cooking Tips

After preparing freezer meals for several months, you'll start developing shortcuts and tricks of your own that make cooking simpler and faster. I've collected a small sampling of assorted helpful tips from experienced freezer-meal cooks to help you:

★ Pour soup or liquid items into freezer bags easily by fitting the bag inside a large empty coffee can. Fold the open edges of the bag down over the top edges of the can and pour the liquid into the bag. One freezer-meal cook sets up a half-dozen coffee cans on her counter, lines the cans with bags, and then moves down the counter, pouring soup into each can.

★ Double-bag soupy items if you're uncertain about the quality of your freezer bags. You can slip a note card with the label and reheating instructions between the two bag layers. The outer bag can also be reused many times.

★ Wear short sleeves so you're not dragging your cuffs through spaghetti sauce or taco meat.

★ Keep a small, damp kitchen towel hooked to your apron for wiping hands and cleaning small spills easily.

★ Keep hot pads readily available and make certain the pads don't get wet or even damp.

★ Keep pets away from your food preparation areas. I've heard horror stories about busy cooks turning around to find a pet eating from a large bowl of meatloaf mix or spaghetti sauce.

★ Wear a hairnet. Professional cooks usually wear a hairnet under a chef's hat to ensure that their hair stays out of the food. Try this at home.

★ Wear an apron with large pockets if you want to keep your frequently used utensils handy. Keep your freezer labels and marking pens in the pockets, too. One cook mentioned that she uses a tool belt to hold her large ladle, wooden spoons, wire whisks, and other utensils.

★ Give your feet extra support while cooking by wearing hiking boots or nurses' shoes.

★ Wear rubber gloves to bone hot chicken or turkey meat.

★ Play upbeat music.

★ Use your food processor to minimize tears when chopping large quantities of onions. Other suggestions include wearing swimming goggles or welder's goggles or placing the onions in the freezer for ten to fifteen minutes before chopping. Some of the more unusual tips I've heard include burning a candle on the counter next to your cutting board, or holding an unlit matchstick in your mouth while chopping.

Frozen Assets Preparation Steps: A Quick Reminder

1) Choose ten to fifteen favorite recipes, depending on how often you're willing to eat the same meal each month. In order to take advantage of sale prices on meats, cheeses, and other items, check local grocery ads before planning your menu.

2) Use a blank calendar page to plan your meals for the month.

3) Go through your recipes, and write down the exact amount of every ingredient. Then, go through your cupboards and refrigerator, marking off each item you have in stock. The remaining ingredients will be your shopping list.

4) Figure out what type of and how many freezer containers you will need. Add to your shopping list any packaging needs you don't already have on hand, such as foil, plastic wrap, disposable foil pans, and freezer bags of varying sizes.

5) Clean out your freezer and refrigerator ahead of time to make room for all the food you'll bring home from the grocery store.

6) Go shopping. After you've arrived home, put away all perishable

foods in your refrigerator, leaving out canned goods and other items needed for cooking the next day.

7) Separate your recipes according to the dishes' main protein ingredient: chicken, ground beef, dried beans, and ham, for example. Plan on preparing the recipes in groups according to main ingredients.

8) Read through your recipes, and break them down into steps. Plan to do similar steps together. If you'll need to brown ground beef for tacos, spaghetti sauce, and Sloppy Joes, brown all the meat together, and then divide the browned meat up for different recipes.

9) Set your freezer to −10 degrees Fahrenheit before you start adding large amounts of unfrozen food to your freezer. It's best to do this the day before cooking.

10) Prepare as many of the ingredients ahead as possible. Decide which things to prepare the evening before, such as chopping vegetables, grating cheese, preparing spaghetti sauce, boiling chicken, and browning ground beef.

11) Go to bed early the night before.

12) Eat a good breakfast on cooking day and don't forget to stop for lunch. Take frequent mini-breaks.

13) Dress comfortably, wear supportive shoes, tie back long hair, put on an apron, and smile.

14) Assemble all necessary utensils, pots, pans, measuring cups, and appliances.

15) Prepare your most complicated recipes early in the day, while you're still fresh.

16) Keep the sink filled with warm, soapy water, and wash your pots and pans, measuring cups, spoons and other cooking utensils as you go. Wash your hands frequently, especially after handling raw meats.

17) Slightly undercook foods for reheating after freezing. This prevents overcooking or a warmed-over taste.

18) Cool food quickly before placing it in the freezer. Food should be no warmer than room temperature when put into the freezer. Freeze food quickly to avoid the formation of large ice crystals.

19) Label all freezer bags and containers with the name of the meal, the date it was frozen, the number of servings, heating instructions, and any other special preparation instructions.

20) Package grated cheese or crumb toppings in small freezer bags, tape them to the main-dish container, and include instructions on the label for adding the topping before reheating.

21) Remove air from your freezer bags either by pressing the air out with your hands, starting at the bottom and working upward, or by using a drinking straw to draw out excess air before sealing.

22) Pack food in quantities for family-sized meals.

23) Pack freezer containers tightly, without air pockets, but remember to leave a head space of at least 1 inch to allow for the expansion of liquid-based meals.

24) Set meal packages directly on freezer shelves, allowing room for air circulation. After the meals are frozen solid, stack them tightly.

So there you have it, the "ins" and "outs" of freezer-meal cooking. Now it's time to put all of these ideas into practice with one of our menu plans, or to design your own! The next three chapters will offer meal plans you can easily follow for your first bulk-cooking experiences. The sections following the meal plans offer recipes you can use and customize to create your own menus and plans. Whether you try our plans or create your own, happy infrequent cooking!

5
★ ★ ★

THE THIRTY-DAY
MEAL PLAN

Freezer-meal cooking can actually become a way of life and can affect more than just meal preparation. I never have to think twice about providing a meal to someone with a new baby or someone facing difficult circumstances. I don't have to worry about what time we get home from the zoo in order to get dinner prepared on time.

Regularly cooking for the freezer can also alter the way you think about food. Every new recipe I see is automatically sent through my mind's "but will it freeze?" filter. Some freezer-meal cooks have been known to choose recipes strictly because the food would look "pretty" in the freezer bag.

Even the family of the freezer-meal cook can take on a new mind-set. The other night my husband was tucking our seven-year-old son in bed. They were reading a story about frozen woolly mammoths found in Siberia. Our son asked, "How'd the mammoth get frozen, Daddy? Did a hunter shoot it and then freeze the meat to eat later?"

My husband chuckled, and said, "Yes, those were the first freezer-meals like Mommy makes—cook for a day, eat for a year!" We laughed about that for days!

The Thirty-Day Meal Lineup

Spaghetti Sauce:

    Sauce over pasta (2 meals)

    Lazy Lasagna (2 meals)

    Baked Ziti (3 meals)

    Meatball Sandwiches (1 meal)

Ground Beef Mixture for Meatloaf and Meatballs:

    Meatloaves (2 meals)

    Salisbury Steak (1 meal)

    Sweet-Sour Meatballs (1 meal)

    Chili-Day Meatballs (1 meal)

    (Meatball sandwiches—listed under Spaghetti Sauce heading)

Chicken Broccoli:

    Served with rice (2 meals)

    Served over noodles (2 meals)

    Mexi-Chicken (3 meals)

    Broccoli-Ham Bake (2 meals)

    Scalloped Potatoes and Ham (4 meals)

    Mix-n-Match Chicken Soup (4 meals)

Thirty-Day Meal Plan Ingredient List

    2 pounds Italian bulk sausage

    9 pounds ground beef

    3 chickens

    3 pounds ham

    ★ ★ ★

    6 onions

    2 green bell peppers

1 bunch celery

4 cloves garlic (or 4 teaspoons minced garlic)

4 pounds broccoli

5 pounds potatoes

1 cup mushrooms

★ ★ ★

Salt

Pepper

Thyme

Oregano

Marjoram

Beef bouillon

Brown sugar

Cornstarch

Flour

Cider vinegar

Lemon juice

Soy sauce

Vegetable oil

Olive oil

2 packages taco seasonings or ground cumin and chili powder

★ ★ ★

5 (15-ounce) jars spaghetti sauce

56 ounces tomato sauce

4 (16-ounce) cans Italian-style stewed tomatoes

2 (16-ounce) cans whole kernel corn

1 (4-ounce) can sliced black olives

2 (10¾-ounce) cans cream of mushroom soup

1 (10¾-ounce) cans cream of broccoli soup

24 ounces chicken broth

1 (14-ounce) can pineapple tidbits or chunks

1 (5-ounce) can water chestnuts

1 (12-ounce) jar chili sauce

11 ounces grape jelly

★ ★ ★

3 pounds dried spaghetti (4 meals' worth)

3 pounds dried ziti or penne pasta

12 ounces lasagna noodles

1½ pounds broad egg noodles

2 cups quick or regular barley

3 cups dry breadcrumbs

3 pounds uncooked rice

★ ★ ★

5 cups mozzarella cheese

¾ cup grated Parmesan cheese

2 cups small-curd cottage cheese or ricotta cheese

½ cup sour cream

1½ cups margarine or butter

12 cups milk

4 pounds Cheddar cheese

6 hoagie rolls or hot dog buns

7 large eggs

2 pounds frozen french fries

Corn tortilla chips or flour tortillas

Thirty-Day Meal Preparation Instructions

The Day Before

★ Shop.

★ Make spaghetti sauce according to directions in the recipe. Cool. Place sauce in refrigerator overnight.

★ Boil chicken(s) in a large Dutch oven or stockpot with enough water to fully cover the chicken. Add several stalks of celery and some sliced onion. Cook until the meat is white to the bone and falls off the bone easily. Cool the cooked chicken slightly, and refrigerate overnight to cool completely.

★ Chop onions, celery, and 1 green bell pepper. Set aside in separate covered bowls in the refrigerator.

★ Cut broccoli into bite-sized pieces. Store in the refrigerator.

Cooking Day

★ Cook ziti according to package directions. It's better to under-cook, rather than overcook, the pasta. The ziti should still be slightly firm, or it will turn to mush after freezing, thawing, and reheating.

★ Prepare Baked Ziti according to directions in the recipe.

★ Cook barley for Mexi-Chicken.

★ Prepare Lazy Lasagna according to directions in the recipe.

★ Bag, label, and freeze leftover spaghetti sauce for use in meatball sandwiches and to serve over pasta.

★ Prepare beef mixture for meatloaves and meatballs according to directions in the recipes.

★ Divide mixture in half.

★ Use half of the mixture to form 1-inch-round meatballs.

★ Use the remaining meat to form two loaves for meatloaves and six thin oval meat patties for Salisbury steak.

★ Bake meatloaves, and cook Salisbury Steak patties according to directions in the recipes.

★ Skim fat off the chicken stock using a slotted spoon. Remove the chicken from the stock and save the stock to make soup later. Bone the chicken and cut the meat into bite-sized pieces.

★ Steam broccoli until just tender.

★ While the broccoli is steaming, prepare the Mexi-Chicken according to directions in the recipe.

★ Prepare Chicken Broccoli according to directions in the recipe.

★ Cut ham into bite-sized pieces.

★ Prepare Broccoli-Ham Bake according to directions in the recipe.

★ Prepare Scalloped Potatoes and Ham according to directions in the recipe.

★ Put the stockpot containing the chicken stock on to boil.

★ Prepare "Mix-n-Match Soup" with the chicken stock, adding any leftover vegetables, meats, grains, or pastas. If you need more liquid, use 1 chicken bouillon cube per 1½ cups added water.

★ Let the soup cook while you're cleaning the kitchen.

★ Allow the soup to cool. Pour the soup into labeled and double-bagged freezer bags and freeze.

Recipes for the
Thirty-Day Meal Plan

Bulk Spaghetti Sauce

SERVES 36

———◆◆◆◆———

Use this sauce over pasta, with Lazy Lasagna and Baked Ziti, and for Meatball
Sandwiches.

 2 tablespoons vegetable oil

 2 pounds Italian bulk sausage

 2 cups chopped onions

 ½ cup chopped green pepper

 ½ cup chopped celery

 2 teaspoons minced garlic

 5 (14-ounce) jars commercial spaghetti sauce or 12 cups
   homemade sauce

 4 (16-ounce) cans Italian-style stewed tomatoes, cut up and undrained

 1 (15-ounce) can sliced black olives

Heat the oil in a large Dutch oven or stockpot over medium heat, and brown
the sausage, onions, green pepper, celery, and garlic. Add the spaghetti sauce
and stewed tomatoes. Reduce the heat to medium-low, and cook for at least
1 hour. Stir occasionally. Add the black olives, and stir. Allow to cool. Set
aside the sauce needed for other recipes, and freeze the remainder in bags for
future pasta meals.

Lazy Lasagna

SERVES 10

When preparing lasagna for the freezer, there's no need to precook the noodles. To make this meal incredibly rich, add one (8-ounce) package cream cheese. Pinch off nickel-sized portions of cream cheese and plop them evenly over the lasagna just before adding the second layer of uncooked pasta.)

12 ounces dried lasagna noodles

2 cups cream-style cottage cheese or ricotta

12 ounces mozzarella cheese, sliced or grated

5 to 6 cups spaghetti sauce

½ cup grated Parmesan cheese

Grease two 10 × 6 × 2-inch baking dishes. Make layers in the following order in each dish: noodles, cottage cheese, mozzarella slices, spaghetti sauce, and Parmesan cheese. Repeat. Make certain the dry noodles are completely covered by sauce. Wrap the pans completely with foil, label, and freeze.

To Serve

Thaw the frozen meal in the refrigerator at least 24 hours before serving. Preheat the oven to 350 degrees.

To serve, keep the lasagna tightly covered and bake for about 45 minutes, or until the edges are bubbly and the center is hot. Remove the cover during the final 10 minutes of cooking. Remove from the oven, and let stand 10 minutes before serving.

Baked Ziti

SERVES 18

———— ◆ ◦ ◆ ◦ ◆ ————

This is one of those recipes my family never seems to eat often enough. Everyone loves it, even my three-year-old. "More yummy noodles, Mommy!" Note that you can substitute 3 cups All-Purpose Ground Meat Mixture (see page 70) for the ground beef cooked with the onion and green pepper.

> 3 pounds dry ziti or penne pasta
>
> 2 tablespoons vegetable oil
>
> 1 pound ground beef (optional)
>
> 1 cup chopped onion
>
> 1 cup chopped green pepper
>
> 2 jars commercial spaghetti sauce (or 6 cups homemade)
>
> 3 cups grated mozzarella cheese
>
> ¾ cup grated Parmesan cheese (to be used at serving time—not during initial prep)

Cook pasta until just barely tender; drain thoroughly, and rinse with cold water to stop the cooking. Heat the oil in a stockpot over medium heat, and brown the ground beef, if using; drain off most of the fat. Add the onion and green pepper, and sauté until the vegetables soften. Add about 2 tablespoons olive oil when sautéing, if needed. Stir in the spaghetti sauce. Add the cooked pasta, mixing well. Divide the mixture into three gallon-sized freezer bags; label each. Divide the grated mozzarella cheese into three quart-sized freezer bags; attach to the pasta bags. Freeze.

To Serve

Thaw the frozen meal in the refrigerator at least 24 hours before serving.

Preheat the oven to 350 degrees.

To serve, spread the pasta into a 9 × 13-inch baking pan. Sprinkle the mozzarella cheese evenly over the pasta. Sprinkle ¼ cup Parmesan cheese over top. Cover the dish with foil and bake for 30 minutes, or until bubbly on the edges and hot in the middle. Remove the foil, and bake 5 more minutes.

Beef Mix for Meatloaf, Salisbury Steaks, and Meatballs

2 Meatloaves

1 meal of Salisbury Steak

3 meals of Meatballs

- Sweet-Sour Meatballs
- Chili-Day Meatballs
- Meatball Sandwiches (also listed under spaghetti sauce)

24 ounces tomato sauce

3 cups dry breadcrumbs

7 eggs, lightly beaten

1 cup diced onion

½ cup diced green bell pepper

2 teaspoons salt, optional

¼ teaspoon dried thyme, crushed

¼ teaspoon dried marjoram, crushed

8 pounds ground beef

Combine the first eight ingredients in a large mixing bowl. Add the ground beef, and mix well. Divide the meat mixture in half.

For Meatloaf

Preheat the oven to 350 degrees. Shape half the meat mixture into three loaves, and place them in a large high-sided baking dish. Don't allow the loaves to touch while baking. Bake for 1 hour. Cool; wrap each in heavy-duty foil. Label them, and freeze.

Thaw the frozen meatloaf in the refrigerator at least 24 hours before serving.

To serve, preheat the oven to 350 degrees. Bake for 30 minutes, or until heated through.

For Meatballs

Preheat the oven to 350 degrees. Shape into meatballs; use a small cookie scoop, if available. Place the meatballs on a broiler pan so the fat can drain while cooking. Bake, uncovered, for 30 minutes. Divide the balls into meal-sized portions. To prevent them from freezing into a solid meatball mass, freeze the meatballs on cookie sheets, and when solid, place them in freezer bags. Label them, and freeze.

Thaw the frozen meatballs in the refrigerator at least 24 hours before serving.

To serve, reheat them with your choice of sauce.

For Salisbury Steak

Form the remaining meat mixture into oval ½-inch-thick patties. Heat a nonstick skillet over medium heat until hot. Place the patties into the skillet; cook, turning once, 7 to 8 minutes, or until the centers are no longer pink. Cool, and place in freezer bags. Label them, and freeze.

Thaw the frozen patties in the refrigerator at least 24 hours before serving.

To serve, reheat them and pour 1 (10¾-ounce) can cream of mushroom soup over top as a sauce. Serve with rice or noodles.

The following recipes show various ways to use frozen meatballs. The sauces require some preparation, but the meals go together quickly with your stockpile of precooked meatballs in the freezer.

Sweet-Sour Meatballs

SERVES 5

1 (14-ounce) can pineapple tidbits or chunks, undrained

¼ cup brown sugar

2 tablespoons cornstarch

¼ cup cider vinegar

1 teaspoon soy sauce (to taste)

1 family meal-sized portion of freezer meatballs

1 (5-ounce) can water chestnuts, drained and thinly sliced

1 green bell pepper, cut in strips

Drain pineapple tidbits, reserving the syrup. In a saucepan, combine the brown sugar and cornstarch. Blend in the reserved syrup, ½ cup water, cider vinegar, and soy sauce. Cook over low heat, stirring, until thick and bubbly. Carefully stir in the meatballs, water chestnuts, green pepper strips, and pineapple. Heat to boiling. Serve over hot rice.

Chili-Day Meatballs

SERVES 5

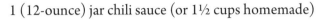

1 (12-ounce) jar chili sauce (or 1½ cups homemade)

11 ounces grape jelly

2 tablespoons lemon juice

1 cube beef bouillon, dissolved in ½ cup water

1 family meal-sized portion of freezer meatballs

Whisk together chili sauce, grape jelly, lemon juice, and bouillon, breaking up all clumps. Cook over low heat until the sauce starts to thicken. Add the meatballs, and continue to cook in the sauce until the meatballs are fully thawed and heated through. Serve over cooked noodles or rice.

Crockpot Method

Mix together the sauce as directed above. Place the frozen meatballs in the crockpot, pouring the sauce over them. Stir gently to coat. Cook for 8 hours on a low setting.

Meatball Sandwiches

SERVES 6

1 family meal-sized serving of meatballs, about 4 to 5 meatballs
    per person

2 cups spaghetti sauce

6 hot dog buns or hoagie rolls

6 thin slices mozzarella cheese

Thaw the frozen meatballs and spaghetti sauce in the refrigerator at least 24
hours before serving.

To Serve

Reheat the meatballs and the spaghetti sauce separately. Place the meatballs
into warmed buns. Ladle a small amount of spaghetti sauce on to each sandwich, and top with a slice of mozzarella.

Mexi-Chicken

SERVES 18

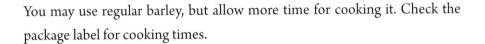

You may use regular barley, but allow more time for cooking it. Check the package label for cooking times.

2 tablespoons vegetable oil

2 cups chopped onions

2 cloves garlic, minced (to taste)

2 cups quick-cooking barley

2 (16-ounce) cans chopped tomatoes, undrained

2 (16-ounce) cans tomato sauce

3 cups chicken broth

2 (16-ounce) cans whole kernel corn, drained

6 cups chopped or shredded cooked chicken

2 packages taco seasoning or 2 tablespoons chili powder and 1 teaspoon ground cumin

Heat the vegetable oil in a Dutch oven over medium heat. Add the onion and garlic and sauté until softened. Add the remaining ingredients, except the chicken, plus 4 cups water. Bring to a boil. Reduce the heat to low, and cook 10 minutes, stirring occasionally. Add the chicken and continue cooking for another 10 minutes, or until the chicken is heated through and the barley is tender. Cool. Spoon the mixture into freezer bags. Label them, and freeze.

To Serve

Thaw the chicken mixture in the refrigerator at least 24 hours before serving.

To serve, reheat the chicken mixture in a skillet over medium heat until heated through. Serve over corn tortilla chips or scoop into flour tortillas and eat fajita-style.

Chicken Broccoli

SERVES 16

1 cup (2 sticks) margarine or butter

1 cup all-purpose flour

8 cups milk

Salt and freshly ground black pepper, to taste

4 cups chopped cooked chicken

2 pounds broccoli, trimmed and steamed

2 pounds Cheddar cheese, grated

Melt the margarine in a large saucepan over medium-low heat. Whisk in the flour, stirring constantly. When mixture begins to boil, whisk in the milk, mixing constantly; add the salt and pepper. As it begins to boil, remove from the heat, and let cool slightly.

Divide the chicken equally among four 8 × 8-inch baking pans. Divide the broccoli equally, and lay it over the chicken. Top each serving with the sauce, and sprinkle ½ cup grated cheese over each portion. Wrap each pan with foil. Label them, and freeze. Alternatively, use zip-top freezer bags, but divide and store the grated cheese in separate small bags in the freezer.

To Serve

Thaw the chicken mixture in the refrigerator at least 24 hours before serving. Preheat the oven to 350 degrees.

To serve, bake the chicken for 30 minutes. Serve over cooked rice or over spaghetti for a Tetrazzini-style meal.

Broccoli-Ham Bake

SERVES 12

2 pounds frozen french fries

4 cups cooked chopped broccoli

1 (10¾-ounce) can cream of mushroom soup

1 (10¾-ounce) can cream of broccoli soup

2 cups milk

2 to 3 cups cubed ham

2 cups grated Cheddar cheese

Spray two 9 × 13-inch baking dishes with nonstick cooking spray. Spread the frozen french fries evenly in the prepared baking dishes. Sprinkle the chopped broccoli over the fries.

In a separate bowl, blend the soups and milk. Stir in the ham, and pour the mixture over the fries and broccoli. Wrap each baking dish with foil. Label them, and freeze. Divide the grated cheese into 2 small freezer bags, and attach to each a baking dish. Label them, and freeze.

To Serve

Thaw the broccoli mixture in the refrigerator at least 24 hours before serving. Preheat the oven to 350 degrees.

To serve, sprinkle the grated cheese over the casserole. Bake for 25 to 30 minutes.

Scalloped Potatoes and Ham

SERVES 20

The potatoes will start to turn brown if you don't get them right into the bags with the sauce, so move quickly when preparing this meal.

5 pounds potatoes, sliced, with skin on

½ cup margarine

½ cup flour

4 cups milk

Salt and freshly ground black pepper, to taste

2 tablespoons vegetable oil

1 pound ham, cubed

1 large onion, chopped

1 pound Cheddar cheese, grated

Put the potatoes into a large saucepan with water to cover. Bring to a boil over medium heat, and cook the potatoes until slightly firm. Drain.

Meanwhile, melt the margarine in a large saucepan over medium-low heat. Whisk in the flour, stirring constantly. When the mixture begins to boil, whisk in the milk, mixing constantly; add the salt and pepper. As it begins to boil, remove from the heat, and let cool slightly.

In a separate pan, heat the vegetable oil over medium heat, and sauté the ham and onions for about 5 minutes. Set aside to cool slightly.

Divide the potatoes evenly among five freezer bags. Divide the ham and onion mixture into equal portions, and add to the potatoes. Divide the sauce equally, and pour over the ham mixture. Label them, and freeze. Divide grated cheese among smaller freezer bags, attach, and freeze.

To Serve

Thaw the potato mixture in the refrigerator at least 24 hours before serving. Preheat the oven to 350 degrees.

To serve, pour into a baking pan, and sprinkle with grated cheese. Bake for 20 minutes, or until heated through.

"Mix-n-Match" Chicken Soup

SERVES 10

10 cups chicken stock, or 4 chicken bouillon cubes dissolved in 10
cups water

Chopped and cooked chicken or turkey

Starch: Choose 2 cups each of one or two items.

Rice, cooked

Barley, cooked

Pasta, dried

Corn kernels

Dumplings (add at end of cooking time)

Vegetables: Choose 1 to 2 cups each of two or more cut–up vegetables.

Carrots	Turnips
Celery	Parsnips
Cabbage	Corn kernels
Onion	Zucchini
Potatoes	Green pepper
Tomatoes	Peas or pea pods
Green beans	Cauliflower
Yellow wax beans	Broccoli

Seasonings: Use 1 to 2 teaspoon(s) of two to four seasonings, or to taste; remember that dried herbs are more potent than fresh ones.

Basil	Oregano
Cayenne pepper, ground	Parsley
Chives	Rosemary
Cumin, ground	Thyme
Garlic	Onion powder
Marjoram	

To Prepare the Soup

Bring stock to boil in large stockpot or Dutch oven. Add all ingredients, and season with salt and pepper, to taste. Reduce the heat to low, and cook for at least 1 hour.

To Freeze

Allow the soup to cool. Use a zip-top freezer bag held over the stockpot, or line a large, empty coffee can with a plastic bag. Use a cup measure to scoop the soup from the stockpot into bags. If you use pasta or rice, add these after adding the liquid, or package and freeze these separately, and add them when you are ready to serve the meal. Label them, and freeze.

THE TWO-WEEK MEAL PLAN

With day-to-day schedules being so varied, people have many reasons for using a two-week meal plan. Sometimes you may not have a full seven or eight hours for preparation on your designated cooking day. In that case, the two-week plan offers a nice alternative and requires only two or three hours of preparation time. And this plan is good for several other reasons: A small budget may not permit buying a month's worth of food at one time. You may not have enough freezer space. It's easier to follow than the four-week plan. Yet this plan lets you enjoy the benefits of bulk cooking.

Two-Week Meal Lineup

All–Purpose Ground Meat Mixture
    Stuffed Peppers (2 meals)
    Sloppy Joes (1 meal)
    Texas-Style Chili (2 meals)
    Poor Man's Casserole (1 meal)

Spaghetti Pie (1 meal)

Black Beans and Rice (2 meals)

Chicken Curry (2 meals; serve with East–Indian Rice Ring)

Broccoli Quiche (1 meal)

Lentil–Rice Soup (2 meals)

Two-Week Meal Plan Ingredient List

5 pounds ground meat, beef or turkey

1 chicken

★ ★ ★

1 pound broccoli

2 apples

8 medium potatoes

5 cups celery

6 cloves of garlic

7 onions

13 large green bell peppers

7 cloves garlic

Lettuce

Tomato

40 ounces salsa

★ ★ ★

Chili powder

Oregano

Cumin, ground

Salt

Pepper

Paprika

Curry powder

Nutmeg, ground

Brown sugar

Cornstarch

Soy sauce

★ ★ ★

7 large eggs

6 cups cheddar cheese

Parmesan cheese

1 cup cottage cheese

1 cup sour cream

1 cup butter or margarine

7 cups milk

★ ★ ★

64 ounces tomato juice

32 ounces tomato sauce

1 (6-ounce) can tomato paste

3 (10¾-ounce) cans tomato soup

4 (16-ounce) cans crushed tomatoes

1 (16-ounce) can Italian-style stewed tomatoes

4 (16-ounce) cans red kidney beans

2 (16-ounce) cans black beans

3 (16-ounce) cans corn kernels

2 (3-ounce) cans sliced mushrooms

★ ★ ★

2 cups dried lentils

6 ounces dried spaghetti

3 pounds long-grain rice

Prepared mustard

¼ cup slivered almonds

½ cup light raisins

Shredded coconut

6 hamburger buns

★ ★ ★

1 pound frozen mixed vegetables

20 ounces frozen corn kernels

Two-Week Plan Preparation Instructions

Day Before

★ Shop.

★ Boil chicken(s) in a large Dutch oven or stockpot with enough water to fully cover the chicken. Add several stalks of celery and some sliced onion. Cook until the meat is white to the bone and falls off the bone easily. Cool cooked chicken slightly, and refrigerate overnight to cool completely. Chop celery, onions, and 1 green bell pepper, reserving other peppers whole for the Stuffed Peppers recipe.

★ Cut up broccoli into bite-sized pieces.

Cooking Day

★ Prepare 4 cups of cooked rice.

★ Meanwhile, cook spaghetti (for Spaghetti Pie) according to package directions. Cook until just tender but not soft. Drain.

★ Peel potatoes. Boil until soft. Drain, mash, and cool. Refrigerate until preparing Poor Man's Casserole.

★ Prepare All-Purpose Ground Meat Mixture according to directions in the recipe.

★ Prepare Sloppy Joes according to directions in the recipe.

★ Prepare Stuffed Peppers according to directions in the recipe.

★ Prepare Texas-Style Chili according to directions in the recipe.

★ Prepare Poor Man's Casserole according to directions in the recipe.

★ Prepare Spaghetti Pie according to directions in the recipe.

★ Prepare Broccoli Quiche according to directions in the recipe.

★ Prepare Black Beans and Rice according to directions in the recipe.

★ Prepare Lentil-Rice Soup according to directions in the recipe.

★ Skim fat off the chicken stock using a slotted spoon. Remove the chicken from the stock. Save the stock to make soup later. Bone the chicken and cut the meat into bite-sized pieces.

★ Prepare Chicken Curry according to directions in the recipe.

★ If there is chicken broth and meat left over at this point, prepare Mix-n-Match Chicken Soup (page 61) while cleaning your cooking area.

Recipes for the Two-Week Meal Plan

All-Purpose Ground Meat Mixture

MAKES ABOUT 12 CUPS

5 pounds ground meat, beef or turkey

2 cups chopped celery

1 clove garlic, minced

2 cups chopped onion

1 cup diced green bell pepper

1 teaspoon salt (optional)

½ teaspoon pepper

Brown the meat in a Dutch oven or large stockpot over medium heat. Drain off the fat. Stir in the celery, garlic, onion, green pepper, salt, and pepper. Cover and cook about 10 minutes, or until the vegetables are tender but not soft.

Sloppy Joes

SERVES 4 TO 6

◆◆◆◆◆

2 cups All-Purpose Ground Meat Mixture (page 70)

1 (10¾-ounce) can tomato soup

2 tablespoons brown sugar

1 teaspoon prepared mustard

Put the All-Purpose Ground Meat Mixture into a large skillet. Add the tomato soup, brown sugar, and mustard, stirring well. Cover the skillet, and heat the mixture over medium-low heat for 10 minutes. Cool slightly. Spoon the mixture into a zip-top freezer bag. Label it, and freeze.

To Serve

Thaw the meat mixture in the refrigerator at least 24 hours before serving. Preheat the oven to 350 degrees.

To serve, heat Sloppy Joe mix in a skillet. Ladle it on to hamburger buns, and serve.

Stuffed Peppers

SERVES 12

2 cups All-Purpose Ground Meat Mixture (page 70)

2 cups cooked rice, preferably long-grain

2 teaspoons paprika

4 cloves garlic, minced

24 ounces tomato sauce

2 (10¾-ounce) cans tomato soup (save until serving day)

Preheat the oven to 350 degrees.

Mix together the All-Purpose Ground Meat Mix, rice, seasonings, and tomato sauce. Stuff the mixture into hollowed-out green bell peppers. Place in roasting pan, and cover with foil.

Bake for 40 minutes. Cool, and wrap each in foil. Label them, and freeze.

To Serve

Thaw the peppers in the refrigerator at least 24 hours before serving. Preheat the oven to 350 degrees.

To serve, unwrap the stuffed peppers, and put them in a roasting pan. Pour the tomato soup over the peppers. Bake for 25 minutes. Alternatively, unwrap the peppers, put them in a microwave-safe dish, pour the tomato soup over top, and reheat.

Texas-Style Chili

SERVES 12

4 cups All-Purpose Ground Beef Mixture (page 70)

2 packages taco seasonings, or 2 tablespoons chili powder plus 2 tablespoons ground cumin

2 teaspoons salt (optional)

4 (16-ounce) cans crushed tomatoes, undrained

4 (16-ounce) cans red kidney beans, drained (or use cooked dried beans)

3 (16-ounce) cans corn kernels

Put all the ingredients into a large pot, and bring to a boil over medium heat. Reduce the heat to low, and cook for at least 1 hour, stirring occasionally. Cool. Spoon the mixture into freezer bags. Label them, and freeze.

To Serve

Thaw in covered saucepan over low heat. After thawed, increase heat and cook until chili is hot.

Poor Man's Casserole

SERVES 6

2 cups All-Purpose Ground Beef Mixture (page 70)

1 pound frozen vegetables, any combination

Seasonings, such as marjoram, parsley, Italian seasoning, or ground
black pepper

3 cups mashed potatoes

1 cup grated Cheddar cheese

Combine the meat, vegetables, and seasonings, and spoon into a 9 × 13-inch baking dish. Spread the mashed potatoes over the top, and sprinkle the potatoes with the cheese. Wrap the dish in foil. Label it, and freeze.

To Serve

Thaw the dish in the refrigerator at least 24 hours before serving. Preheat the oven to 350 degrees.

To serve, uncover the dish, and bake for 20 to 30 minutes, or until heated through.

Spaghetti Pie

SERVES 6

6 ounces dried spaghetti

2 tablespoons butter or margarine

½ cup grated Parmesan cheese

2 eggs, well beaten

1 cup cottage cheese

2 tablespoons vegetable oil

½ pound ground beef

½ cup chopped onion

1 (8-ounce) can Italian-style stewed tomatoes, undrained

1 (6-ounce) can tomato paste

1 teaspoon sugar

1 teaspoon dried oregano, crushed

½ clove garlic, minced

½ cup shredded cheese, such as mozzarella, Cheddar, Monterrey Jack, or American

Cook pasta until just barely tender; drain thoroughly and rinse with cold water to stop the cooking. Stir the butter into the spaghetti. Stir in the Parmesan cheese and eggs.

Grease a 9-inch pie plate. Line it with the pasta mixture as a crust, and spread the cottage cheese over top.

Heat the vegetable oil in a skillet over medium heat, and sauté the ground beef and onions until the meat is browned. Drain. Add tomatoes, tomato paste, sugar, oregano, and garlic. Cook until heated through. Spoon the meat mixture into the crust. Sprinkle the grated cheese over all, and wrap the pan with foil. Label it, and freeze.

To Serve

Thaw the pie in the refrigerator at least 24 hours before serving. Preheat the oven to 350 degrees.

To serve, keep the pie covered with foil, and bake for 25 minutes. Remove the foil, and bake for 5 minutes more, or until the cheese is lightly browned.

Broccoli Quiche

SERVES 6

Consider freezing single slices of the quiche to enjoy for lunch or dinner. It can be served hot or cold.

Crust

　　　　1 to 2 cups cooked rice

　　　　1 egg, beaten

　　　　1 teaspoon soy sauce

Filling

　　　　1 to 2 cups cut-up cooked broccoli

　　　　4 eggs, beaten

　　　　1½ cups milk, or light cream

　　　　½ teaspoon salt (optional)

　　　　⅛ teaspoon pepper

　　　　Dash of ground nutmeg or ground mace

　　　　1 cup grated cheese, such as Swiss, Cheddar, or American

Preheat the oven to 350 degrees. Spray a 9-inch pie plate with nonstick cooking spray.

To make the crust, mix together the rice, the 1 egg, and the soy sauce. Spread evenly in the prepared pan. Bake for 10 minutes. Remove from the oven.

To make the filling, layer the broccoli on the crust. Mix together the remaining eggs, milk, salt, pepper, and nutmeg, and pour over the broccoli. Top with the grated cheese. Bake for 45 minutes, or until set. Remove from the oven. Cool, and wrap the pie pan with foil. Label it, and freeze.

Black Beans and Rice

SERVES 8

2 cans black beans, drained

20 ounces frozen corn kernels

2 cups uncooked long-grain rice

32 ounces salsa (mild, medium, or hot)

3 cups tomato juice

½ teaspoon ground cumin

½ teaspoon dried oregano

2 cups grated Cheddar cheese

Preheat the oven to 375 degrees.

Combine all the ingredients except the cheese in a large bowl. Spoon into two casserole dishes. Bake, covered, for 1 hour. Remove from the oven. Cool, and wrap in foil. Label it, and freeze. Divide the grated cheese into two portions, and put them into small freezer bags. Attach, and freeze.

To Serve

Thaw one of the containers in the refrigerator at least 24 hours before serving. Preheat the oven to 350 degrees.

To serve, sprinkle the grated cheese over the top. Bake for 15 to 20 minutes, or until the cheese has melted and the beans and rice are heated through.

Lentil-Rice Soup

SERVES 10

1 (12-ounce) can tomato paste

2 (16-ounce) cans tomatoes, undrained

2 cups uncooked lentils

2 cups uncooked rice

2 medium onions, chopped

1 cup chopped celery

2 cloves garlic, minced

Salt and pepper, to taste

Put tomato paste and canned tomatoes into large Dutch oven or stockpot. Add 8 cups water, and stir in the remaining ingredients. Bring the mixture to a boil over medium heat. Reduce the heat to low, and cook for about 1 hour, or until the lentils and rice are tender. Allow the soup to cool.

Use a zip-top freezer bag held over the stockpot, or line a large, empty coffee can with a plastic bag. Use a cup measure to scoop the soup from the stockpot into bags. If you use pasta or rice, add these after adding the liquid, or package and freeze these separately, and add them when you are ready to serve the meal. Label them, and freeze.

To Serve

Thaw the soup in the refrigerator at least 24 hours before serving. To serve, reheat it in a large saucepan.

Chicken Curry

SERVES 10

Serve Chicken Curry over hot cooked rice and pass condiments, such as raisins, shredded coconut, chopped peanuts, and chutney; or serve it in the East-Indian Rice Ring (page 82).

2 tablespoons butter

2 cups diced apple

2 cups sliced celery

1 cup chopped onion

2 cloves garlic, minced

4 tablespoons cornstarch

4 to 6 teaspoons curry powder (or to taste)

1 teaspoon salt (optional)

1½ cups cold chicken broth

4 cups milk

4 cups cooked chicken, diced

2 (3-ounce) cans, or 1 cup fresh, sliced mushrooms, drained

In a large saucepan, melt the butter, and add the apple, celery, onion, and garlic. Sauté until the onion is translucent.

Mix together the cornstarch, curry powder, salt, and broth. Stir the cornstarch mixture into the onion mixture; add the milk. Cook and stir until the mixture thickens and bubbles. Stir in the chicken and mushrooms, and cook until heated through. Cool, and divide the mixture into freezer bags. Label them, and freeze.

To Serve

Thaw the curry in the refrigerator at least 24 hours before serving. To serve, pour the mixture into a saucepan, and reheat thoroughly.

East-Indian Rice Ring

Prepare on serving day.

    ¼ cup butter

    ½ cup chopped onion

    ¼ cup slivered almonds

    ½ cup golden raisins

    6 cups hot steamed rice

    Chicken Curry (page 80)

    Shredded coconut (optional)

Grease a 6½-cup ring mold; set aside. Melt the butter in a skillet over medium heat, and sauté the onions and almonds until golden. Add the raisins, and cook until plumped. Stir in the rice until well blended. Press mixture into the ring mold. When ready to serve, unmold the rice onto a round serving platter. Fill the center of the ring with Chicken Curry. Garnish with shredded coconut, if desired.

THE TEN-DAY HOLIDAY MEAL PLAN

Could you imagine a relaxed Christmas and New Year without needing to cook any main dinner recipes, and only side dishes and desserts? If that sounds like a great gift to give yourself this year, plan ahead this holiday season using my Ten-Day Holiday Meal Plan.

This plan covers the main-dish dinner recipes from just before Christmas until New Year's Day. Many people find they need larger amounts of food during this time of year because guests and unexpected visitors drop in, or college-age children return home for the holidays. If these recipes prepare more than you'll be needing, you can serve leftovers for lunches, or divide the recipes into additional freezer pans and stretch the meals out for a longer period of time.

These recipes include main dishes for a holiday dinner of turkey; several meals of planned turkey leftovers; a breakfast casserole that can be served on Christmas or New Year's morning; and recipes that could be used for company meals throughout the holidays.

Now that you can plan ahead and get your cooking out of the way, get ready to relax and enjoy the holidays!

Ten-Day Holiday Meal Lineup

Turkey Dinner (serves however many you need)

Turkey-Rice (serves 8)

Turkey Stuffed Manicotti (serves 12)

Turkey Noodle Soup (serves 8 to 10)

Ground Beef Mixture

Texas-Style Chili (serves 12)

Easy Taco Salads (serves 6 to 8)

Spaghetti Sauce

Baked Ziti (serves 18)

Lazy Lasagna (serves 10)

Pasta with sauce (serves 10)

Broccoli-and-Ham Bake (serves 12)

Ham-and-Cheese Quiche (serves 24)

Holiday Breakfast Casserole (serves 8)

Holiday Meal Plan Ingredients List

Turkey (determine turkey size according to recipe directions on page 92)

2 pounds bulk Italian sausage

Ham (2 to 3 pounds)

2½ pounds ground beef or turkey

1 pound bulk sausage

★ ★ ★

8 onions

6 carrots

1 large bunch celery

2 green bell peppers

4 cups broccoli

1 head iceberg lettuce

2 tomatoes

1 bunch green onions

★ ★ ★

Olive oil

Bay leaves

Salt

Pepper

Sage

Thyme

Garlic

Oregano

2 packages taco seasoning (or ground cumin and chili powder)

Bunch fresh parsley

Rosemary

Dry mustard

★ ★ ★

7 (15-ounce) jars commercial spaghetti sauce

64 ounces Italian-style stewed tomatoes

2 (4-ounce) cans sliced black olives

5 (10¾-ounce) cream of mushroom soup

1 (10¾-ounce) cream of broccoli soup

16 ounces salsa (mild, medium, or hot)

64 ounces crushed tomatoes

64 ounces red kidney beans

32 ounces tomato sauce

★ ★ ★

16 ounces lasagna noodles

16 manicotti shells

12 ounce wide egg noodles

2 pounds dried ziti or penne pasta

★ ★ ★

1 bottle white wine

★ ★ ★

5 cups yellow cheese

2 cups cottage cheese

5 cups mozzarella cheese

3 cups Parmesan cheese

2 cups ricotta cheese

7 large eggs

★ ★ ★

6 ounces frozen peas

2 pounds frozen french fries

One large bag corn chips or tortilla chips

★ ★ ★

Long-grain rice

Bread

★ ★ ★

Heavy-duty wide aluminum foil

Holiday Preparation Instructions
[Three half-days, including shopping]

Day One

★ Shop.

★ Make spaghetti sauce according to recipe. Cool; place sauce in refrigerator overnight.

★ Peel and quarter three onions.

★ Cut six celery stalks into 2-inch pieces.

★ Cut two carrots into 2-inch pieces.

★ Chop remaining onions, celery, and green bell peppers. Separate, cover, and refrigerate chopped vegetables.

★ Cut broccoli into bite-sized pieces, and refrigerate.

★ Dice and refrigerate ham.

★ Cook 4 to 5 cups rice, cover, and refrigerate.

Day Two

★ First thing in the morning, prepare and roast the turkey according to the recipe. After roasting, cover it with foil, and refrigerate it overnight.

★ While the turkey is roasting, cook the pasta according to package directions, but undercook it slightly; drain.

★ Prepare the Lazy Lasagna according to directions in the recipe. Label it, and freeze.

★ Prepare Baked Ziti according to directions in the recipe. Label it, and freeze.

★ Pour remaining spaghetti sauce into two freezer bags. Label it, and freeze.

★ Prepare All-Purpose Ground Meat Mixture according to directions in the recipe.

★ Prepare Broccoli-Ham Bake according to directions in the recipe while the All-Purpose Ground Meat Mixture is cooking. Label it, and freeze.

★ Divide the cooked All-Purpose Ground Meat Mixture into two portions: put 2 cups into a large skillet and the remaining 4 cups into a Dutch oven or stockpot.

★ Prepare the All-Purpose Ground Meat Mixture in the skillet as taco filling for Taco Salads. Label it, and freeze.

★ Prepare as the remaining meat as Texas-Style Chili according to directions in the recipe. Label it, and freeze.

★ Prepare the Ham-and-Cheese Quiche. Label it, and freeze.

★ Cook the manicotti shells until just tender; drain. Carefully place the shells into a shallow pan. Cover, and refrigerate overnight.

Day Three

★ Remove turkey from the refrigerator. Carefully slice turkey to prepare for turkey dinner meal. Freeze sliced turkey according to directions in the recipe. Set aside 8 cups of diced turkey for the planned "leftover" recipes. Use any additional turkey meat in the Turkey Noodle Soup recipe on page 110.

★ Remove all meat from bones.

★ Begin preparing soup stock by putting the bones and assorted remaining pieces into a large stockpot or Dutch oven. Fill pot with water to cover. Add several stalks of celery, and bring the liquid to a boil. Reduce the heat to low, and cook for at least 1 hour.

★ Meanwhile, prepare the Turkey Rice according to directions in the recipe. Label it, and freeze.

★ Prepare the Turkey-Stuffed Manicotti according to directions in the recipe. Label it, and freeze.

★ Prepare the Holiday Breakfast Casserole according to directions in the recipe. Label it, and freeze.

★ Strain the turkey stock, reserving the meat in a separate bowl. Refrigerate the stock to cool. When the fat has congealed on top, skim off the fat with a slotted spoon.

★ Prepare Turkey Noodle Soup according to directions in the recipe. Cool, label it, and freeze.

Recipes for the Ten-Day Holiday Meal Plan

Turkey Dinner

You'll need a minimum 6-pound turkey for enough leftover turkey after the main dinner. For the main turkey dinner, add ¾ pound per person to the 6 pounds already required for the leftover recipes.

Number of People = Weight of Turkey

6 people = 10½ pounds

8 people = 12 pounds

10 people = 13½ pounds

12 people = 15 pounds

14 people = 16½ pounds

16 people = 18 pounds

18 people = 19½ pounds

20 people = 21 pounds

To Prepare Turkey

3 onions, quartered, divided

6 sliced celery stalks, divided

2 medium sliced carrots

2 bay leaves

1½ cups white wine or water

Turkey, rinsed, dried, and giblets removed

1 tablespoon olive oil

2 teaspoons salt

2 teaspoons pepper

2 teaspoons dried sage

1 teaspoon dried thyme

Canned chicken broth, 1 cup per pound (reserve until time to freeze meat)

Preheat the oven; see roasting chart below.

Put 2 quartered onions, 4 celery stalks, carrots, bay leaves, and white wine in the bottom of a deep roasting pan. Stuff turkey loosely with the remaining onion and celery stalks. Mix the olive oil with the salt, pepper, sage, and thyme, and brush the turkey with the mixture. Cover turkey loosely with a large sheet of foil coated lightly with olive oil, crimping foil onto edges of roasting pan. Cook according to chart below. During last 45 minutes, cut band of skin or string between legs and tail. Uncover and continue roasting until done. Baste if desired.

TURKEY ROASTING CHART (TURKEY LOOSELY WRAPPED WITH FOIL)

12 to 16 lbs / 325 degrees / 4 to 5 hours

16 to 20 lbs / 325 degrees / 5 to 6 hours

20 to 24 lbs / 325 degrees / 6 to 7 hours

TESTING FOR DONENESS

About 20 minutes before the end of the roasting time, test the turkey for doneness. The skin on the thickest part of the drumstick should feel soft when squeezed between your fingers, the drumstick should move freely, and the meat thermometer inserted into thickest part of leg should read 185 degrees.

FREEZING INSTRUCTIONS

Pour all meat juices from the roasting pan into a bowl, and remove the vegetables. Chill the juices until the fat firms. Skim the fat off the turkey juices using a slotted spoon. Pour the remaining juices into a freezer bag. Label it, and freeze. Allow the turkey to cool in the pan for about 30 minutes; refrigerate the turkey to cool it completely. When fully chilled, slice the turkey, removing all meat from the bones. Put the breast and dark meat into freezer bags, reserving 8 cups of diced turkey meat for the "leftover" recipes. Pour chicken broth into bags over the meat. Label them, and freeze.

To Serve

Thaw a bag of meat and broth and a bag of turkey drippings in the refrigerator at least 24 hours before serving. Preheat the oven to 350 degrees.

To serve, place the meat into a baking dish, cover it, and bake for 30 minutes. Alternatively, place the turkey and broth into a microwave-safe dish, cover it with plastic wrap, and heat according to manufacturer's directions. Drain off the broth, reserving it to make more gravy, if needed. Arrange the heated turkey slices attractively on a platter. Serve.

Gravy Instructions

SERVES 12

If needed, add additional water, chicken broth, or white wine to equal 3 cups.

> 2 tablespoons butter or margarine
>
> ½ cup white wine
>
> ⅓ cup all-purpose flour
>
> ½ teaspoon salt (optional)
>
> 3 cups thawed turkey drippings

Melt the butter in a saucepan over medium heat. Stir in the flour and salt, if using. Reduce the heat to medium-low, and cook until bubbly, stirring constantly. Slowly stir the turkey drippings into the butter mixture, and continue stir while increasing the heat to medium. Cook until the mixture boils, and reduce the heat to low, stirring and cooking 2 minutes more.

Bulk Spaghetti Sauce

SERVES 36

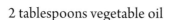

2 tablespoons vegetable oil

2 pounds Italian bulk sausage

2 cups chopped onions

½ cup chopped green pepper

½ cup chopped celery

2 teaspoons minced garlic

5 (14-ounce) jars commercial spaghetti sauce or 12 cups homemade sauce

4 (16-ounce) cans Italian-style stewed tomatoes, cut up and undrained

1 (15-ounce) can sliced black olives

Heat the oil in a large Dutch oven or stockpot over medium heat, and brown the sausage, onions, green pepper, celery. Add the spaghetti sauce and stewed tomatoes. Reduce the heat to medium-low, and cook for at least 1 hour. Stir occasionally. Add the black olives, and stir. Allow to cool. Set aside the sauce needed for other recipes, and freeze the remaining in bags for future pasta meals.

Lazy Lasagna

SERVES 10

When preparing lasagna for the freezer, there's no need to precook the noodles. To make this meal incredibly rich, add one (8-ounce) package cream cheese. Pinch off nickel-sized portions of cream cheese and plop them evenly over the lasagna just before adding the second layer of uncooked pasta.

½ teaspoon dried oregano

6 cups spaghetti sauce

12 ounces dried lasagna noodles

2 cups cream-style cottage cheese or ricotta

12 ounces mozzarella cheese, sliced or grated

½ cup grated Parmesan cheese

Stir the oregano into the spaghetti sauce. Grease two 10 × 6 × 2-inch baking dishes. Make layers in the following order in each dish: noodles, cottage cheese, mozzarella slices, spaghetti sauce, and Parmesan cheese. Repeat. Make certain the dry noodles are completely covered by sauce. Wrap the pans completely with foil; label and freeze.

To Serve

Thaw the frozen meal in the refrigerator at least 24 hours before serving. Preheat the oven to 350 degrees.

To serve, keep the lasagna tightly covered, and bake for about 45 minutes, or until the edges are bubbly and the center is hot. Remove the cover during the final 10 minutes of cooking. Remove from the oven, and let stand 10 minutes before serving.

Baked Ziti

SERVES 18

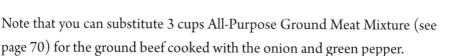

Note that you can substitute 3 cups All-Purpose Ground Meat Mixture (see page 70) for the ground beef cooked with the onion and green pepper.

> 3 pounds dry ziti or penne pasta
>
> 1 pound ground beef (optional; see note above)
>
> 1 cup chopped onion
>
> 1 cup chopped green pepper
>
> 2 jars commercial spaghetti sauce (or 6 cups homemade)
>
> 3 cups grated mozzarella cheese
>
> ¾ cup grated Parmesan cheese (to be used at serving time—not during initial prep)

Cook pasta until just barely tender; drain thoroughly and rinse with cold water to stop the cooking.

Heat a stockpot over medium heat, and brown the ground beef, if using; drain off most of the fat. Add the onion and green pepper, and sauté until vegetables soften; add about 2 tablespoons olive oil when sautéing, if needed. Stir in the spaghetti sauce; add the cooked pasta, mixing well. Divide the mixture into three gallon-sized freezer bags; label each. Divide the grated mozzarella cheese into three quart-sized freezer bags; attach to the pasta bags. Label them, and freeze.

To Serve

Thaw the frozen meal in the refrigerator at least 24 hours before serving.

Preheat the oven to 350 degrees.

To serve, spread the pasta into a 9 × 13-inch baking pan. Sprinkle the mozzarella cheese evenly over the pasta. Sprinkle ¼ cup Parmesan cheese over top. Cover the dish with foil, and bake for 30 minutes, or until bubbly on the edges and hot in the middle. Remove the foil, and bake 5 more minutes.

Broccoli-Ham Bake

SERVES 12

2 pounds frozen french fries

4 cups chopped cooked broccoli

1 (10¾-ounce) can cream of mushroom soup

1 (10¾-ounce) can cream of broccoli soup

2 cups milk

2 to 3 cups cubed ham

2 cups grated Cheddar cheese

Spray two 9 × 13-inch baking dishes with nonstick cooking spray. Spread the frozen french fries evenly in the prepared baking dishes. Sprinkle the chopped broccoli over the fries.

In a separate bowl, blend the soups and milk. Stir in the ham, and pour the mixture over the fries and broccoli. Wrap each baking dish with foil. Label them, and freeze. Divide the grated cheese into 2 small freezer bags, and attach to each baking dish.

To Serve

Thaw the broccoli mixture in the refrigerator at least 24 hours before serving. Preheat the oven to 350 degrees.

To serve, sprinkle grated cheese over the casserole. Bake for 25 to 30 minutes.

Ham-and-Cheese Quiche

SERVES 6

Consider freezing single slices of the quiche to enjoy for lunch or dinner. It can be served hot or cold.

Crust

> 1 to 2 cups cooked rice
>
> 1 egg, beaten
>
> 1 teaspoon soy sauce

Filling

> 1 to 2 cups cut-up cooked broccoli
>
> 4 eggs, beaten
>
> 1½ cups milk or light cream
>
> ½ teaspoon salt (optional)
>
> ⅛ teaspoon pepper
>
> Dash of ground nutmeg or ground mace
>
> 1 cup grated cheese, such as Swiss, Cheddar, or American

Preheat the oven to 350 degrees. Spray a 9-inch pie plate with nonstick cooking spray.

To make the crust, mix together the rice, 1 egg, and soy sauce. Spread evenly in the prepared pan. Bake for 10 minutes. Remove from the oven.

To make the filling, layer the broccoli on the crust. Mix together the remaining eggs, milk, salt, pepper, and nutmeg, and pour over the broccoli.

Top with the grated cheese. Bake for 45 minutes, or until set. Remove from the oven. Cool, and wrap the pie pan with foil. Label it, and freeze.

All-Purpose Ground Meat Mixture

2½ pounds ground meat, beef, or turkey

1 cup chopped celery

1 clove garlic, minced

1 cup chopped onion

½ cup diced green pepper

½ teaspoon salt (optional)

¼ teaspoon pepper

Brown the meat in a Dutch oven or large stockpot over medium heat. Drain off the fat. Stir in the celery, garlic, onion, green pepper, salt, and pepper. Cover and cook about 10 minutes, or until the vegetables are tender but not soft.

Easy Taco Salads

1 package taco seasonings

2 cups cooked All-Purpose Ground Beef Mixture (see page 70)

1 large bag corn chips or tortilla chips

Lettuce, shredded

2 cups grated cheese

2 tomatoes, diced

2 green onions, sliced

1 (4-ounce) can black olives (optional)

1 cup sour cream

8 ounces salsa

Add one package taco seasoning to the All-Purpose Ground Meat Mixture; cook according to package directions, using recommended amount of water from package. On individual plates, place a layer of corn chips or tortilla chips; spoon the taco mixture over the chips. Add a portion of shredded lettuce, grated cheese, diced tomatoes, sliced green onions, sliced black olives, sour cream, and salsa to each plate. Serve.

Texas-Style Chili

SERVES 12

4 cups All-Purpose Ground Beef Mixture (page 70)

2 tablespoons chili powder

2 tablespoons ground cumin

2 teaspoons salt (optional)

4 (16-ounce) cans crushed tomatoes, undrained

4 (16-ounce) cans red kidney beans, drained (or use cooked dried
   beans)

3 (16-ounce) cans corn kernels

Put all the ingredients into a large pot, and bring to a boil over medium heat. Reduce the heat to low, and cook for at least 1 hour, stirring occasionally. Cool. Spoon the mixture into freezer bags. Label them, and freeze.

To Serve

Thaw in covered saucepan over low heat. After thawed, increase heat and cook until chili is hot.

Turkey-Stuffed Manicotti

SERVES 8

I've found that cooling the manicotti shells completely before stuffing them makes the stuffing process much easier than attempting when the noodles are hot. I've also discovered that using a long-handled infant-feeding spoon with a tiny bowl works perfectly for stuffing the shells.

2 tablespoons butter, melted

4 cups cooked chopped or shredded turkey

2 cups ricotta cheese

Ground black pepper, to taste

½ cup grated Parmesan cheese

2 green onions, chopped

1 teaspoon dried parsley

½ teaspoon dried rosemary

2 eggs, lightly beaten

4 cups tomato sauce or 2 (15-ounce) jars spaghetti sauce

16 manicotti shells, cooked until just barely soft

Heat the butter in a large skillet over medium heat, and brown the turkey for 2 to 4 minutes. Stir in the ricotta, black pepper, Parmesan cheese, green onions, parsley, rosemary, and eggs. Mix well. Cover the bottom of baking pans with 1 cup tomato sauce. Stuff the manicotti shells with the turkey mixture, and place in them in the baking pans. Pour in the remaining sauce. Cover the baking pans with foil. Label them, and freeze.

To Serve

Thaw the frozen meal in the refrigerator at least 24 hours before serving.

Preheat the oven to 350 degrees.

To serve, sprinkle ½ cup Parmesan cheese over the manicotti. Bake, uncovered, for 35 minutes, or until bubbly and hot in the center.

Turkey Rice

SERVES 12

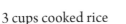

3 cups cooked rice

4 cups cooked, chopped turkey

2 small onions, chopped

1 cup chopped celery

2 cups grated Cheddar cheese

4 (10¾-ounce) cans cream of mushroom soup

Salt and pepper, to taste

Mix together all the ingredients in a large bowl. Divide the mixture between two 9 × 13-inch casserole dishes. Cover each with foil. Label them, and freeze. Alternatively, divide the mixture into two freezer bags. Label them, and freeze.

To Serve

Thaw the frozen meal in the refrigerator at least 24 hours before serving.

Preheat the oven to 350 degrees.

To serve, bake for 30 minutes, or until bubbly and hot in the center.

Holiday Breakfast Casserole

SERVES 8

6 to 8 slices bread, white or whole wheat, crusts removed

1 pound bulk sausage or crumbled links, cooked

1 medium apple, peeled and diced

6 ounces Cheddar cheese, shredded

5 eggs

2 cups milk or half-and-half

1 teaspoon salt

1 teaspoon dry mustard

Lay the bread in the bottom of a 9 × 13-inch ovenproof baking dish. Sprinkle the sausage and chopped apple evenly over the bread. Sprinkle on the cheese. In a bowl, beat together the eggs, milk, salt, and dry mustard. Pour the egg mixture over the bread and sausage. Wrap the pan in foil. Label it, and freeze.

To Serve

Thaw the frozen meal in the refrigerator at least 24 hours before serving.

Preheat the oven to 350 degrees.

To serve, bake for 35 to 40 minutes. Let stand 10 minutes before serving.

Turkey Noodle Soup

SERVES 10

If necessary, add chicken bouillon cubes and water to equal 10 cups—dissolve 1 bouillon cube for every 2 cups of water.

> 10 cups turkey broth
>
> Any leftover turkey pieces or tidbits
>
> 1 cup chopped onion
>
> 1 to 2 cups thinly sliced carrots
>
> 6 ounces frozen peas
>
> 1 teaspoon dried thyme
>
> 1 teaspoon crumbled dried sage
>
> 1 to 2 cloves garlic, minced
>
> 1 teaspoon crumbled dried oregano
>
> Salt and pepper, to taste
>
> 1 tablespoon chopped parsley
>
> 12 ounces dried egg noodles

Bring stock to boil in large stockpot or Dutch oven. Add all the ingredients *except* the noodles. Reduce heat, and simmer 1 hour. Remove from the heat, and add the noodles. Cool the soup completely in refrigerator. Ladle the soup into freezer bags. Label them, and freeze.

MORE MAIN-DISH
DINNER RECIPES

You will find many recipes ideal for freezer cooking in this book, but the book does not contain an exhaustive list of recipes. The following recipes are not necessarily gourmet fare, but they're family favorites that have been tested in the freezer and chosen with the eating habits of real families in mind.

Maybe you'll find some new family favorite recipes in this book. I hope so. I've found that most people who seek out a bulk-cooking method are looking for affordable, simple, and tasty recipes that use common ingredients. Many of these recipes have been adapted from suggestions sent to me via email, and others are family favorites or have been shared by close friends.

Don't be afraid to substitute ingredients or play around with these recipes. Be creative! Rather than changing your eating habits to suit a cooking method, take these meals and this method and suit it to your family's individual tastes and budget. Please feel free to use your own personal recipes or adapt these recipes in any way you desire. Make the recipes lower in fat, or less expensive. You'll find a list of suggestions for reducing fat in recipes in Appendix D.

You'll find several recipes for large batches of sauce or meat mixtures that you can use in a variety of ways. For example, the spaghetti sauce recipe will have a listing of other uses besides the standard "sauce over pasta" meal.

Happy infrequent cooking!

Bulk Spaghetti Sauce

36 SERVINGS

———————◆┤◆├◆———————

Ground beef, turkey, pork, or any combination of ground meats can be used in this recipe, but the recommended Italian sausage is the tastiest. You can also prepare this without meat, or you can substitute TVP.

2 pounds Italian sausage

2 cups chopped onions

½ cup chopped green pepper

½ cup chopped celery

2 teaspoons minced garlic

5 jars commercial spaghetti sauce (or 12 cups homemade sauce)

4 (16-ounce) cans Italian-style stewed tomatoes, cut up, undrained

1 large can sliced black olives

Brown sausage, onion, green pepper, celery, and garlic in large Dutch oven or stockpot. Add spaghetti sauce and stewed tomatoes. Simmer on low to medium heat for at least 1 hour. Stir occasionally. Add black olives after simmering. Allow to cool. Divide into meal-sized portions; pour into labeled freezer bags; freeze.

Suggested Uses for Spaghetti Sauce

★ Serve as sauce over pasta.

★ Use in Lazy Lasagna (page 115).

★ Serve over Meatballs (page 120) with mozzarella cheese on hoagie rolls.

★ Filling for Calzones (page 153).

★ Sauce for Chicken Cacciatore (page 138).

★ Use in Spaghetti Pie (page 118).

★ Use in Baked Ziti (page 117).

Lazy Lasagna

10 SERVINGS

When preparing lasagna for the freezer, there's no need to precook the noodles. If you layer the casserole with dry noodles and ensure your noodles are completely covered with sauce, the noodles will cook during the freezing and baking process, absorbing the sauce.

½ teaspoon dried oregano

6 cups spaghetti sauce

12 ounces lasagna noodles, uncooked

2 cups cream-style small curd cottage cheese, or ricotta

12 ounces mozzarella cheese, sliced or grated

½ cup grated Parmesan cheese

Stir oregano into spaghetti sauce. In two greased 10 × 6 × 2-inch baking dishes, make layers in the following order: half each noodles, cottage cheese, mozzarella slices, spaghetti sauce, and sprinkled Parmesan cheese. Repeat. Make certain the dry noodles are completely covered by sauce. Wrap pans completely with foil; label and freeze.

(To make this meal incredibly rich, add one 8-ounce package cream cheese. Pinch off nickel-sized portions of cream cheese and plop evenly over lasagna just before adding the second layer of uncooked pasta.)

To Serve

To thaw, take meal from freezer at least 24 hours before serving. Place in refrigerator. Bake tightly covered at 350 degrees for about 45 minutes, or until edges are bubbly and center is hot. Take cover off during final 10 minutes of cooking time. Let stand 10 minutes before serving.

Baked Ziti

18 SERVINGS

3 pounds ziti (or penne) pasta

1 pound ground beef (optional)

1 cup chopped onion

1 cup chopped green pepper

2 jars commercial spaghetti sauce (or 6 cups homemade)

3 cups grated mozzarella cheese

¾ cup grated Parmesan cheese (to be used at serving time—not during initial prep)

Note: Three cups All-Purpose Ground Meat Mixture (see page 70) can be substituted for ground beef, chopped onion and green pepper.

Cook pasta until just barely tender; drain thoroughly and rinse with cold water to stop cooking process. Brown ground beef; drain. Add onion and green pepper to meat and sauté until vegetables are softened (if needed, add small amount of olive oil during sauté process). Add spaghetti sauce. Combine sauce and cooked pasta; mix well. Divide sauce and pasta mixture into three gallon-sized freezer bags; label. Divide grated mozzarella into three quart-sized freezer bags; attach to pasta bags. Freeze.

To Serve

Thaw. Spread pasta into 9 × 13-inch baking pan. Sprinkle mozzarella evenly over pasta. Sprinkle ¼ cup Parmesan cheese over top. Cover dish and bake for 30 minutes at 350 degrees, or until bubbly on the edges and hot in the middle. Remove foil and bake 5 more minutes.

Spaghetti Pie

6 SERVINGS

————————◆◗◆◖◆————————

This recipe can easily be double or tripled. The original Spaghetti Pie recipe calls for a full pound of ground beef, but I only use half a pound per pie—I find that's more than enough. This recipe could also be made with ground turkey, Italian sausage, TVP, or without meat.

6 ounces dry spaghetti noodles

2 tablespoons butter or margarine

½ cup Parmesan cheese

2 eggs, beaten well

½ pound ground beef

½ cup chopped onion

1 (8-ounce) can Italian-style stewed tomatoes, undrained

1 (6-ounces) can tomato paste

1 teaspoon sugar

1 teaspoon dried oregano, crushed

½ clove garlic, minced

1 cup cottage cheese

½ cup shredded cheese (your choice: mozzarella, cheddar, American, or Monterrey Jack)

(One cup All-Purpose Ground Meat Mixture (page 70) can be substituted for ground beef and chopped onion, and 1½ cups bulk spaghetti sauce can be substituted for tomatoes, tomato paste, and spices. If using pre-made ingredients, mix the spaghetti sauce and meat mixture together and heat through. Follow all other directions below.)

Cook spaghetti noodles. Drain. Stir margarine into hot noodles until melted. Stir in Parmesan cheese and eggs. Form pasta mixture into a crust-shape in a buttered 9-inch pie plate. In skillet, cook ground beef and onions until meat is browned. Drain. Add tomatoes, tomato paste, sugar, oregano and garlic. Heat through. Spread cottage cheese over bottom of spaghetti crust. Top with tomato and meat mixture. Sprinkle grated cheese over all. Cover pie pan with foil; label and freeze.

To Serve

Thaw. Bake, covered, for 25 minutes at 350 degrees. Remove foil and bake for 5 more minutes or until cheese is lightly browned.

Beef Mix for Meatloaf and Meatballs

3 MEATLOAVES AND 4 MEALS OF MEATBALLS

Cooking up a large batch of this meat mixture goes a long way toward establishing a supply of Frozen Assets. From this one recipe, you can make Meatloaf, Meatballs, and Salisbury Steak. On the pages following this recipe there are ideas for sauces and other plans for serving meatballs. You can pour the various sauces over sliced meatloaf, too.

    24 ounces tomato sauce

    3 cups dry bread crumbs

    7 eggs, lightly beaten

    1 cup finely chopped onion

    ½ cup finely chopped green pepper

    2 teaspoons salt, optional

    ¼ teaspoon dried thyme, crushed

    ¼ teaspoon dried marjoram, crushed

    8 pounds ground beef

Combine first 8 ingredients. Add ground beef and mix well. Divide meat mixture in half.

For Meatloaf

Shape half the meat mixture into three loaves and place in a large high-sided baking dish. Don't allow the loaves to touch while baking. Bake at 350 degrees for 1 hour. Cool, wrap in heavy-duty foil, label, and freeze. To serve, thaw loaves and bake in 350-degree oven for 30 minutes or until heated through.

For Meatballs

Shape into meatballs (use small cookie scoop, if available) and place on broiler pan so grease can drain while cooking. Bake, uncovered, in 350-degree oven for 30 minutes. Divide into meal-sized portions. To prevent from freezing into a solid meatball mass, freeze individually on cookie sheets and then place in freezer bags. Label and freeze. To serve, thaw and reheat with your choice of sauces.

For Salisbury Steak

Form meat mixture into oval ½-inch thick patties. Heat nonstick skillet over medium heat until hot. Place beef patty in skillet; cook 7 to 8 minutes or until centers are no longer pink, turning once. Cool, place in freezer bags, and freeze. Thaw, heat with 1 (10¾-ounce) can cream of mushroom soup poured over as sauce, and serve with rice or noodles.

Assorted Meatball Options

The following recipes are various ways to use frozen meatballs. The sauces require some preparation, but the meals go together quickly with your stockpile of precooked meatballs in the freezer.

★ Meatball Sandwiches (page 54).

★ Sweet-Sour Meatballs (page 123).

★ Chili-Day Meatballs (page 124).

★ East-Indian Meatballs (page 125).

★ Tomato-Sauced Meatballs (page 127).

★ Meatball Stroganoff (page 128).

★ California Meatballs (page 129).

★ Heat in brown gravy and serve with mashed potatoes.

★ Serve on skewers. (Kids love it!)

★ Add to vegetable soup.

Sweet-Sour Meatballs

5 SERVINGS

————◆◆◆————

1 (14-ounce) can pineapple tidbits or chunks, undrained

¼ cup brown sugar

2 tablespoons cornstarch

½ cup water

¼ cup cider vinegar

1 teaspoon soy sauce (or to taste)

1 family meal-sized portion of freezer meatballs

1 (5-ounce) can water chestnuts, drained and thinly sliced

1 green pepper, cut in strips

Drain pineapple tidbits, reserving syrup. In medium saucepan, combine brown sugar and cornstarch. Blend in reserved syrup, water, cider vinegar, and soy sauce. Cook and stir over low heat until thick and bubbly. Carefully stir in meatballs, water chestnuts, green pepper strips, and pineapple. Heat to boiling. Serve over hot cooked rice.

Chili-Day Meatballs

5 SERVINGS

—◆·◆·◆—

1 (12-ounce) jar chili sauce (or 1½ cups homemade)

1 (11-ounce) jar grape jelly

2 tablespoons lemon juice

1 cube beef bouillon dissolved in ½ cup water

1 family meal-sized portion of freezer meatballs

Whisk together chili sauce, grape jelly, lemon juice, and bouillon, breaking up all clumps. Simmer on low heat until sauce starts to thicken. Add freezer meatballs; cook in sauce until meatballs are fully thawed and heated through. Serve over cooked noodles or rice.

Crockpot Method

Mix together sauce as described above. Place frozen meatballs in crockpot, pouring sauce over them. Stir gently to coat. Cook for 8 hours on a low setting.

East-Indian Meatballs

SERVES 5

1 tablespoon butter

1 cup diced apple

1 clove garlic, minced

1 cup sliced celery

½ cup chopped onion

1 cup beef broth

2 tablespoons cornstarch

2 teaspoons curry powder

2 teaspoons sugar

1 family meal-sized portion of freezer meatballs

1 (3-ounce) can sliced or ½ cup fresh mushrooms, sautéed in butter
until soft

Melt the butter in a saucepan. Add the apple, garlic, celery, and onion and cook until the onion is tender. Combine the beef broth, cornstarch, curry powder, and sugar. Stir into the onion mixture. Cook over low heat, stirring until the mixture thickens and bubbles. Stir in the meatballs and mushrooms. Cook until the meatballs are heated through. Serve over hot cooked rice or in the East-Indian Rice Ring (recipe on page 126).

East-Indian Rice Ring

(SERVE WITH EAST-INDIAN MEATBALLS OR CHICKEN CURRY)

¼ cup butter

½ cup chopped onion

¼ cup slivered almonds

½ cup light raisins

6 cups hot cooked rice

Shredded coconut (optional)

In skillet, melt butter and sauté chopped onion and almonds until golden. Add light raisins; heat until plump. Add hot rice; mix gently. Press mixture into greased 6½-cup ring mold. Remove from mold at once and place on to a round serving platter. Fill center of rice ring with East-Indian Meatballs (page 125) or Chicken Curry (page 143). If desired, top with a sprinkling of shredded coconut.

Tomato-Sauced Meatballs

SERVES 5

1 (10¾-ounce) can condensed tomato soup

1 teaspoon Worcestershire sauce

1 family meal-sized portion of freezer meatballs

Mix together the soup, ½ cup water, and Worcestershire sauce. Place the meatballs in a saucepan, and pour the soup mixture over the meatballs. Cook over low heat until the meatballs are heated through. Serve over hot cooked rice.

Meatball Stroganoff

SERVES 5

1 (10¾-ounce) can condensed cream of mushroom soup

½ cup sour cream or plain yogurt

1 cup sliced mushrooms, cooked in butter until soft (optional)

1 family meal-sized portion of freezer meatballs

Mix together the mushroom soup and sour cream. Gently stir in the mushrooms, if using, and meatballs. Cook over low heat until the meatballs are heated through. Serve over hot cooked rice or over egg noodles tossed with melted butter and parsley.

California Meatballs

SERVES 5

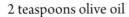

2 teaspoons olive oil

1 medium onion, thinly sliced (optional)

1 family meal-sized portion of freezer meatballs

1 bottle Catalina salad dressing

Heat the olive oil in a large skillet over medium heat, and sauté the onion slices, if using, until softened. Put the frozen meatballs into the skillet, and add the salad dressing. Cover the skillet, and cook over low heat until the dressing caramelizes on the meatballs and onion, and the meatballs are fully thawed and heated through. Serve over rice.

All-Purpose Ground Meat Mixture

MAKES ABOUT 12 CUPS

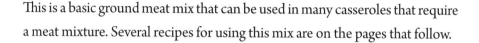

This is a basic ground meat mix that can be used in many casseroles that require a meat mixture. Several recipes for using this mix are on the pages that follow.

> 5 pounds ground meat (beef or turkey)
>
> 2 cups chopped celery
>
> 1 clove garlic, minced
>
> 2 cups chopped onion
>
> 1 cup diced green pepper
>
> 1 teaspoon salt (optional)
>
> ½ teaspoon pepper

In a large pot, brown ground beef. Drain. Stir in celery, garlic, onion, green pepper, salt, and pepper; cover and simmer about 10 minutes, until vegetables are tender but not soft. You can use this mixture immediately during your cooking session or freeze in 2-cup portions for later use.

Suggested Uses (Be Creative)

TACOS: Add 1 package taco seasoning to 2 cups All-Purpose Ground Meat Mixture; follow package directions for amount of water. Freeze. To serve, thaw the meat in the refrigerator for at least 24 hours before using, and reheat taco mixture; prepare tacos as you would normally.

TACO POTATOES: Follow instructions for the taco recipe above, but serve the mixture over baked potatoes instead of tortillas or taco shells. Top with grated cheese, diced tomatoes, sour cream, sliced green onions, sliced black olives, and salsa.

EASY TACO SALADS: Follow instructions for taco mixture. Place a layer of corn chips or tortilla chips on plate, spoon taco mixture over chips, and add layer of shredded lettuce. Add diced tomatoes, sliced green onions, sliced black olives, sour cream, and salsa.

The All–Purpose Ground Meat Mixture can also be used for:
- ★ Stuffed Peppers (see page 132)

- ★ Sloppy Joes (see page 133)

- ★ Texas-Style Chili (see page 134)

- ★ Spaghetti Pie (see page 118)

- ★ Baked Ziti (see page 48)

Stuffed Peppers

12 SERVINGS

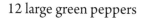

12 large green peppers

2 cups All-Purpose Ground Meat Mix (page 70) (or brown together
    1 pound ground beef, 2 cups chopped onion, and 2 cloves
    minced garlic)

2 cups cooked rice (long-grain is best, but use what you have)

2 teaspoon paprika

24 ounces tomato sauce

2 (10¾-ounce) cans tomato soup (save until serving day)

Cut off tops of green peppers and remove seeds. Mix together All-Purpose
Ground Meat Mixture, rice, spices, and tomato sauce. Stuff meat and rice
mixture into green peppers. Place in roasting pan. Bake, covered, at 350 degrees for 40 minutes. Cool. Wrap individually in foil, label, and freeze.

To Serve

Unwrap stuffed peppers. Place in roasting pan. Pour tomato soup over
peppers. Heat at 350 degrees for 25 minutes, or unwrap and cook in
microwave oven.

Sloppy Joes

4–6 SERVINGS

This is a simple recipe that is easy to double or triple. My family loves sloppy joes. (Must be something about the fact that for once, it's okay to be messy while eating.)

2 cups All-Purpose Ground Meat Mixture (page 70) (or brown together 1 pound ground beef and 1 small chopped onion)

1 (10¾-ounce) can tomato soup

2 tablespoons brown sugar

1 teaspoon prepared mustard

Place All-Purpose Ground Meat Mixture into large skillet. Add tomato soup, brown sugar, and mustard; stir. Cover and simmer 10 minutes. Freeze.

To Serve

Thaw and heat Sloppy Joe mix in skillet. Serve ladled on to hamburger buns.

Texas-Style Chili

12 SERVINGS

4 cups All-Purpose Ground Meat Mixture (page 70)

2 tablespoons chili powder

2 tablespoons ground cumin

2 teaspoons salt (optional)

4 (16-ounce) cans crushed tomatoes, undrained

4 (16-ounce) cans red kidney beans, drained (or use home prepared
beans)

3 cans corn

Place all ingredients into large pot. Bring to a boil. Reduce heat and simmer for at least 1 hour, stirring occasionally. Cool chili. Put into freezer bags; label and freeze.

To Serve

Thaw in covered saucepan over low heat. After thawed, increase heat and cook until chili is hot.

Poor Man's Casserole

6 SERVINGS

———◆◆◆———

2 cups All-Purpose Ground Beef Mixture (page 70)

1 pound frozen vegetables (your choice, any combination)

Spices (whatever you like: marjoram, parsley, Italian seasoning, ground pepper, etc.)

3 cups mashed potatoes

1 cup yellow grated cheese

Mix meat with vegetables and place in 9 × 13-inch casserole dish. Add spices. Spread mashed potatoes over top of meat and vegetable mixture. Sprinkle grated cheese over top of potatoes. Wrap casserole in foil, label, and freeze.

To Serve

Thaw. Heat uncovered in 350-degree oven for 20 to 30 minutes, or until heated through.

Mexi-Chicken

18 SERVINGS

2 cups chopped onion

2 cloves garlic (or to taste), minced

2 tablespoons vegetable oil

4 cups water

2 cups Quaker Quick barley (regular barley can be used, but cooking time increases dramatically)

2 (16-ounce) cans chopped tomatoes, undrained

2 (16-ounce) cans tomato sauce

3 cups chicken broth

2 (16-ounce) cans whole kernel corn, drained

6 cups cooked, chopped chicken

2 packages taco seasonings, or 2 tablespoons chili powder and 1 teaspoon cumin

In large Dutch oven, cook onion and garlic in oil until tender. Add all ingredients except chicken. Bring to boil. Reduce heat and simmer 10 minutes, stirring occasionally. Add cooked chicken; continue simmering for another 10 minutes, or until chicken is heated through and barley is tender. Cool, spoon into freezer bags, label, and freeze.

If you're using regular barley, rather than the quick cooking variety, you'll need to cook the barley ahead of time. Allow 1 hour for barley to cook. Follow directions on the barley package.

To Serve

Thaw chicken mixture. Heat in skillet until hot. Serve over corn tortilla chips or scoop into flour tortillas, fajita-style.

Chicken Cacciatore

SERVES 15

This recipe can also be made with whole chicken pieces. Bake the individual chicken pieces before freezing. Prepare the sauce without the chicken. Pour the sauce into freezer bags; add the cooked chicken pieces. Label them, and freeze. Thaw in the refrigerator for 24 hours. To serve, heat in a skillet until the chicken pieces are heated through.

> 1 tablespoon olive oil
>
> 2 medium onions, thinly sliced
>
> 1 green pepper, thinly sliced
>
> 1½ cups mushrooms, sliced
>
> 2 cloves (or 2 teaspoons) garlic, minced
>
> 3 cups cooked, cubed chicken
>
> 6 cups homemade spaghetti sauce or 2 (15-ounce) jars of commercial sauce plus 1 can Italian-style stewed tomatoes

Heat the oil in a large skillet or Dutch oven over medium heat, and sauté the onions, green pepper, mushrooms, and garlic until the onions are soft. Stir in the chicken and spaghetti sauce. Reduce the heat to low, and cook for 15 minutes. Cool. Store in freezer bags. Label them, and freeze.

To Serve

Thaw the chicken mixture in the refrigerator at least 24 hours before serving.

To serve, pour the chicken into a saucepan, and reheat it over medium-low heat until heated through. Serve over egg noodles, spaghetti, or rice. Sprinkle with Parmesan cheese, if desired.

Chicken Casserole

SERVES 12

Note: Instead of mayonnaise, substitute salad dressing if you plan to freeze this dish. Save the potato chips for when you plan to serve.

5 cups cooked, diced chicken

5 cups chopped celery

1 bunch green onions, white and green parts sliced

1 (5¾ -ounce) can sliced olives

1 cup slivered almonds

2 cups grated Cheddar cheese

1 cup mayonnaise   *or salad dressing if freezing*

1 cup sour cream

2 cups crushed potato chips

Grease two 8 × 8-inch baking pans. Combine the chicken, celery, green onions, olives, and almonds in a large bowl. Stir in 1 cup cheese. In a separate bowl, mix the mayonnaise and sour cream, and stir into the chicken mixture. Spoon the mixture into the prepared pans. Wrap with foil and label. Divide the remaining cheese into 2 small freezer bags, label them, and attach to each baking dish. Freeze.

To Serve

Thaw the chicken mixture in the refrigerator at least 24 hours before serving. Preheat the oven to 350 degrees.

To serve, sprinkle the baking dish with potato chips and top with the cheese. Bake, uncovered, for 25 minutes, or until heated through.

South-of-the-Border Chicken Bake

SERVES 18

2 (10¾-ounce) cans cream of mushroom soup

2 (10¾-ounce) cans cream of chicken soup

3½ cups milk

4 cups cooked chopped chicken

2 onions, diced

2 cups salsa (mild, medium, or hot)

4 cups grated Cheddar cheese

24 corn tortillas, each cut into eighths

Lightly grease three 8 × 8-inch baking pans. Combine the soups and milk in a large bowl, stirring well. Add the chicken, onions, salsa, and 3 cups grated cheese. Divide the tortilla pieces into three uniform portions, and layer them in the bottom of each pan. Divide the chicken mixture into three uniform portions, and layer the mixture on the tortillas. Top each pan with grated cheese. Wrap in foil. Label each, and freeze.

To Serve

Thaw the chicken mixture in the refrigerator at least 24 hours before serving. Preheat the oven to 350 degrees.

To serve, bake the chicken for 35 to 45 minutes, or until heated through and bubbly.

Chicken Broccoli

16 SERVINGS

◆◆◆◆◆

1 cup margarine

1 cup flour

8 cups milk

Salt and pepper, to taste

4 cups cooked chicken, chopped

2 pounds broccoli, steamed

2 pounds cheddar cheese, grated

Make white sauce: Melt margarine in a large heavy pan. Add flour, stirring constantly. When it reaches the boiling point, add milk, mixing constantly with a wire whisk. Heat until almost boiling, stirring constantly. Remove from heat. Place cooked chicken into four 8 × 8-inch baking pans. Divide steamed broccoli and place over chicken. Pour white sauce over all. Sprinkle each pan with grated cheese. Cover pans with foil, label, and freeze. This recipe can also be frozen in zip-top freezer bags to conserve space in your freezer. If storing in bags, divide grated cheese among smaller freezer bags and freeze separately from the chicken and broccoli.

To Serve

Thaw. Bake at 350 degrees for 30 minutes. Serve over cooked rice or spaghetti noodles for a Tetrazzini-type meal.

Chicken Creole

SERVES 20

4 tablespoons butter

2 cups chopped onions

2 cups chopped celery

1 (6-ounce) can tomato paste

2 (16-ounce) cans tomatoes, diced

3 tablespoons Worcestershire sauce

1 teaspoon salt

2 teaspoon sugar

1 tablespoon chili powder

Tabasco sauce, to taste

¼ teaspoon unflavored gelatin, dissolved in 2 tablespoons cold water

5 cups cooked diced chicken or 2 pounds shrimp, cooked and peeled

Heat the butter in a Dutch oven over medium heat, and sauté the onions and celery until tender. Stir together the tomato paste and ½ cup water in a bowl until smooth; add this mixture to the onions. Stir in the tomatoes, Worcestershire sauce, salt, sugar, chili powder, and Tabasco. Reduce the heat to low, and cook, uncovered, for 40 minutes. Stir in dissolved gelatin. Remove from heat; cool. Stir in chicken pieces and divide the mixture into uniform portions. Spoon into freezer bags. Label them, and freeze.

Thaw the chicken mixture in the refrigerator at least 24 hours before serving.

To Serve

Heat the chicken in a saucepan until warmed through. Serve with hot cooked rice.

Chicken Curry

10 SERVINGS

2 tablespoons butter

2 cups finely chopped, pared apple

2 cups sliced celery

1 cup chopped onion

2 cloves garlic, minced

4 tablespoons cornstarch

4–6 teaspoons curry powder (or to taste)

1 teaspoon salt (optional)

1½ cups cold chicken broth

4 cups milk

4 cups cooked, diced chicken

2 (3-ounce) cans sliced mushrooms, drained (or 1 cup sliced fresh)

In saucepan, melt butter; add apple, celery, onion and garlic. Cook until onion is tender. In separate bowl, combine cornstarch, curry, salt, and broth. Stir into onion and apple mixture; add milk. Cook and stir until mixture thickens and bubbles. Stir in chicken and mushrooms. Heat through. Divide into freezer bags; label and freeze.

To Serve

Thaw. In saucepan, heat thoroughly. Serve Chicken Curry over hot cooked rice and pass condiments—raisins, shredded coconut, chopped peanuts, chutney—or serve in East-Indian Rice Ring (page 126).

Turkey-Stuffed Manicotti

8 SERVINGS

This is a wonderful way to use up leftover Thanksgiving turkey.

4 cups cooked turkey meat, chopped or shredded

2 tablespoons butter

2 cups ricotta cheese

Ground black pepper, to taste

½ cup Parmesan cheese

2 green onions, chopped

1 teaspoon dried parsley

½ teaspoon dried rosemary

2 eggs, lightly beaten

4 cups tomato sauce

16 manicotti shells, cooked until just barely softened

In large skillet, brown turkey for 2 to 4 minutes. Mix turkey with ricotta. Add pepper, Parmesan, green onions, parsley, rosemary, and egg; mix well. Cover bottom of baking pans with 1 cup of the tomato sauce. Stuff manicotti shells with turkey mixture; place in baking pans and cover with remaining sauce. Cover baking pans with foil, label, and freeze.

To Serve
Thaw. Sprinkle ½ cup Parmesan cheese over manicotti. Bake, uncovered, at 350 degrees for 35 minutes, or until hot and bubbly.

Turkey Rice

12 SERVINGS

---

3 cups cooked rice

4 cups cooked turkey, chopped

2 small onions, chopped

1 cup chopped celery

2 cups grated yellow cheese

4 (10¾-ounce) cans cream of mushroom soup

Salt and pepper, to taste

In large bowl, mix together all ingredients. Divide between two 9 × 13-inch casserole dishes. Cover with foil; label and freeze.

To Serve

Thaw. Bake at 350 degrees for 30 minutes, or until bubbly and hot in the center.

Crab-and-Swiss Quiche

SERVES 6

———◆◆◆———

This recipe freezes well and can easily be doubled or tripled. My quiche recipes usually call for a rice crust. I've found that pastry crusts sometimes get soggy when frozen, but I've never had that problem with a rice crust. Feel free to substitute a pastry shell for the rice crust, if you desire. This recipe can be made with either canned crabmeat or imitation crabmeat. I've received just as many compliments when I use the imitation crab. You could also substitute cooked shrimp for the crabmeat.

Crust

> 2 cups cooked white or brown rice
>
> 1 egg, beaten
>
> 1 teaspoon soy sauce

Filling

> 4 ounces Swiss cheese, grated
>
> 1 (7.5-ounce) can crabmeat, drained and flaked, or 8 ounces imitation crabmeat
>
> 2 green onions, green and white parts, sliced
>
> 4 eggs, beaten
>
> 1½ cups light cream or part-skim milk
>
> ½ teaspoon salt (optional)
>
> ½ teaspoon grated lemon peel
>
> ¼ teaspoon dry mustard

Dash ground nutmeg or ground mace

⅛ cup sliced almonds

Crust

Preheat the oven to 350 degrees. Butter a quiche pan or a pie plate.

To make the crust, mix together the rice, egg, and soy sauce. Pat evenly into the prepared pan. Bake for 10 minutes. Remove from the oven.

Meanwhile, to make the filling, layer the cheese onto the rice crust. Top with the crabmeat, and sprinkle with the green onions. Mix together the eggs, milk, salt, lemon peel, mustard, and nutmeg. Pour over the cheese, and garnish with the almonds. Bake for 45 minutes, or until set. Remove from the oven, and let sit 10 minutes before slicing and serving. Alternatively, wrap the quiche in foil. Label it, and freeze.

To Serve

The cooked quiche can be served cold after thawing for a yummy hot-weather treat, or you can heat the thawed quiche at 350 degrees for 25 minutes.

Basic "Use-It-Up" Quiche

SERVES 6

You can use almost any leftover vegetable or meat in this recipe. If you have eggs, milk, rice, and cheese, you can practically clean out your refrigerator right into your quiche pan. I always add the cheese last when making this quiche. The cheese makes a beautiful mellow-brown crust on the top. I usually add a bit of chopped onion to my quiches for flavor. Broccoli makes an especially nice vegetable quiche.

Crust

> 2 cups cooked white or brown rice
>
> 1 egg, beaten
>
> 1 teaspoon soy sauce

Filling

> ½ pound leftover vegetables, chopped (single vegetable or a mix)
>
> 4 eggs, beaten
>
> 1½ cups milk or light cream
>
> ½ teaspoon salt (optional)
>
> ⅛ teaspoon pepper
>
> Dash nutmeg or ground mace
>
> 1 cup grated cheese, such as Swiss or Cheddar

Preheat the oven to 350 degrees. Butter a quiche pan or a pie plate.

To make the crust, mix together the rice, egg, and soy sauce. Pat evenly into the prepared pan. Bake for 10 minutes. Remove from the oven.

To make the filling, layer the chopped vegetables onto the rice crust. Mix together the eggs, milk, salt, pepper, and nutmeg. Pour over the vegetables, and top with the almonds. Bake for 45 minutes, or until set. Remove from the oven, and let sit 10 minutes before slicing and serving. Alternatively, wrap the quiche in foil. Label it, and freeze.

Suggested Quiche Combinations

★ Quiche Lorraine: cooked and crumbled bacon with Swiss cheese.

★ Chicken Elegante: 1 pound cooked chicken, chopped; ½ cup diced green bell pepper; and ½ cup sliced mushrooms.

★ Spinach: spread 1 pound finely chopped, well-drained cooked spinach over Swiss cheese.

★ Quiche Nicoise: 1 thinly sliced tomato; ⅓ cup sliced ripe olives; and add ¼ teaspoon garlic powder with other spices, omitting the nutmeg.

★ Green Chile and Cheese Pie: 1½ cups Monterrey Jack cheese; 1 (4-ounce) can chopped green chiles; and ⅛ teaspoon ground cumin.

To Serve

The quiche can be served cold after thawing, or heat the thawed quiche at 350 degrees for 20 minutes.

Crustless "Use-It-Up" Quiche

SERVES 6

No pie shell or rice crust is needed. The biscuit mix makes its own crust.

1½ cups milk

½ cup commercial biscuit mix

3 eggs, lightly beaten

¼ teaspoon salt (optional)

⅛ teaspoon pepper

Dash of ground nutmeg or ground mace

½ to 1 cup any cooked chopped vegetable

⅓ cup chopped onion

¾ cup grated cheese

Preheat the oven to 400 degrees. Lightly grease a 9-inch pie pan or quiche dish.

Combine the milk, biscuit mix, eggs, salt, pepper, and nutmeg, and beat until smooth. Pour into the pan. Sprinkle the vegetables and cheese over the egg mixture. Bake for 30 minutes, or until golden brown and a knife inserted near the center comes out clean. Remove from the oven, and let sit 10 minutes before slicing and serving. Alternatively, wrap the quiche in foil. Label it, and freeze.

To Serve
The quiche can be served cold after thawing, or heat the thawed quiche at 350 degrees for 20 minutes.

Stuffed Potato Shells

12 MAIN-DISH SERVINGS OR 24 SIDE-DISH SERVINGS

12 baking potatoes, scrubbed

1 teaspoon salt (optional)

¼ teaspoon pepper (or to taste)

¼ cup margarine or butter

Milk as needed, for mixing

½ cup chopped onion

1½ cups grated Cheddar cheese

1½ cups grated Monterrey Jack cheese

2 boxes frozen chopped spinach, thawed and drained

Bake potatoes at 400 degrees for 1 hour. Remove them from the oven. Slice the hot potatoes in half lengthwise, and carefully scoop out the flesh, leaving a thin potato-skin shell. Mash the flesh with salt, if using, pepper, and margarine; add milk, if needed. Stir in the onion, both cheeses, and spinach. Heap the mixture into the potato shells.

Bake the filled potato shells at 400 degrees for 20 minutes, or until golden brown.

To Freeze

Fill potato shells with the spinach mixture, but don't reheat stuffed potato shells. Freeze the potatoes by placing them on a cookie sheet in the freezer for a few minutes, until they harden. Pack the hardened potato shells into heavy-duty freezer bags. Label them, and freeze.

To thaw the potatoes, remove as many potatoes from the bag as you need. Let them thaw in the refrigerator. Preheat the oven to 400 degrees.

To Serve

Place potatoes on a cookie sheet or in a shallow baking dish. Bake for 20 minutes, or until golden brown.

Calzones

SERVES 12

These are little dough-wrapped baked sandwiches. This recipe for calzone dough can be filled with practically anything: a small amount of spaghetti sauce (a tad too much sauce makes them drippy beyond belief, so use sparingly) and mozzarella cheese, spinach, or broccoli, just to name a few items. Take a look at some of the dough-wrapped freezer sandwiches in the grocery freezer section for more ideas of what to put into these sandwiches. You can also make simple calzones using frozen bread dough from the store.

> 2 tablespoons active dry yeast
>
> 2 cups warm water (but not hot)
>
> 5 cups all-purpose flour
>
> 2 cups cornmeal
>
> 2 tablespoons salt
>
> 5 tablespoons olive oil

Dissolve yeast in the warm water until foamy. Stir in the flour, cornmeal, sugar, salt, and olive oil. Let rise 1 hour.

Preheat the oven to 425 degrees.

Divide the dough into 12 equal balls. Flatten the dough balls into twelve 8-inch rounds. Put the filling on to half of the circle, and fold the other half over top. Pinch the edges to seal shut. Prick the tops several times with fork. Sprinkle cornmeal on to a cookie sheet. Bake the calzones for 18 to 20 minutes. Cool, wrap each individually, label, and freeze.

To Serve

Thaw the calzones in the refrigerator for at least 24 hours before serving.

To serve, reheat the calzones in a hot oven or microwave them.

Suggested Fillings

★ Spaghetti sauce and mozzarella cheese

★ Spaghetti sauce and pepperoni slices

★ Sliced ham with Swiss or Havarti cheese

★ Chopped cooked chicken, cream cheese, and chives

★ Chopped cooked chicken and cooked broccoli pieces

Pizza Shells

Submitted by Gina Dalquest

Premade pizza shells are one of the fastest-selling items at grocery stores. Unfortunately, they are also very expensive. With a little effort, you can make your own and keep a bunch in your freezer for quick dinners or easy snacks.

Pinch sugar

1¼ cups warm milk

2 packages active dry yeast (I use five teaspoons, because I buy yeast in big bags)

3⅓ cups flour

½ teaspoon salt

1 egg

Stir the sugar into the warm milk, and sprinkle with the yeast. Let stand for 5 minutes or until foamy. Stir gently to moisten any dry particles. Sift the flour and salt into a large bowl. Lightly beat the egg into the yeast mixture and pour it into the flour mixture, mixing well to make a dough.

Knead the dough on a floured surface until it is smooth and springy, 5 to 10 minutes. Cover the dough, and let it rise in a warm place for 25 minutes. Divide the dough according to your needs and freezer space. Shape each piece into a ball and, on a floured surface, roll it out to about ½-inch thickness. Place on baking sheets, and freeze for 1 hour. Remove the frozen shells from the baking sheets, wrap them well in plastic wrap or freezer bags, and refreeze. Pizza shells will keep in the freezer for about 1 month.

To Serve

Preheat the oven to 425 degrees. Thaw a shell or shells, top with desired toppings, and bake for about 20 minutes, or until the cheese is melted and just browned.

Broccoli-Ham Bake

12 SERVINGS

2 pound frozen french fries

4 cups cooked, chopped broccoli

1 (10¾-ounce) can cream of mushroom soup

1 (10¾-ounce) can cream of broccoli soup

2 cups milk

2–3 cups cubed ham

2 cups grated yellow cheese (any variety)

Spread frozen french fries in two greased 9 × 13-inch baking dishes. Sprinkle chopped broccoli over fries. In a separate bowl, blend soups and milk, stir in ham, and pour over fries and broccoli. Wrap baking dish, label, and freeze. Place grated cheese in 2 small freezer bags and attach them to the baking dish.

To Serve

Thaw. Sprinkle grated cheese over top of casserole. Bake at 350 degrees for 25 to 30 minutes.

Scalloped Potatoes and Ham

20 SERVINGS

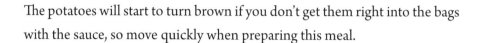

The potatoes will start to turn brown if you don't get them right into the bags with the sauce, so move quickly when preparing this meal.

½ cup margarine

½ cup flour

4 cups milk

Salt and pepper, to taste

1 pound ham, in small cubes

1 large onion, chopped

5 pounds potatoes, sliced, with skin on

1 pound yellow cheese (any variety), grated

For Sauce

Melt margarine in heavy pan. Add flour, stirring constantly.

Heat to a boil. Add milk, mixing constantly with wire whisk. Heat until thickened, stirring constantly. Add spices. In a separate pan, sauté meat with onions. Boil sliced potatoes, but remove from heat while still firm. Divide potatoes between 5 freezer bags. Divide ham and onion mixture, and add to potatoes in freezer bags. Divide white sauce and pour over meat and potatoes in freezer bags. Label and freeze quickly. Divide grated cheese between smaller freezer bags, attach and freeze.

To Serve

Thaw potato mixture. Pour into baking pan. Sprinkle with grated cheese. Bake at 350 degrees for 20 minutes, or until heated through.

Split Pea Soup with Ham

SERVES 8

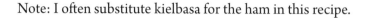

Note: I often substitute kielbasa for the ham in this recipe.

4 cups dried split peas

1 cup diced ham

1 teaspoon salt

½ teaspoon pepper

¼ teaspoon marjoram, crushed

1 bay leaf, crushed

1 cup chopped celery

1 cup chopped onions

1 cup sliced carrots

Rinse the peas thoroughly to remove any grit. Combine the peas, 10 cups water, ham, salt, pepper, and marjoram in a large Dutch oven or stockpot. Bring to a boil. Cover, reduce heat to low, and cook for 1½ hours. Stir occasionally. Add the celery, onion, and carrots. Remove the cover, and cook for 30 minutes. ˜

Lentil-Rice Soup

1 (12-ounce) can tomato paste

2 (16-ounce) cans tomatoes, undrained

8 cups water

2 cups uncooked lentils

2 cups uncooked rice

2 medium onions, chopped

1 cup chopped celery

2 cloves garlic, minced

Salt and pepper, to taste

Put tomato paste and canned tomatoes into large Dutch oven or stockpot. Add water. Stir in all other ingredients. Heat to boiling. Turn down heat and simmer for 1 hour, or until lentils are soft and rice is cooked.

Lentil Ranchero

SERVES 12

1 pound ground beef (optional)

8 cups cooked lentils

2 packages onion soup mix

2 cups catsup

2 teaspoons prepared mustard

2 teaspoons vinegar

Preheat the oven to 400 degrees.

Brown the ground beef, if using, in a large skillet over medium heat; drain off the fat. Stir in the remaining ingredients plus 2 cups water. Pour into two casserole dishes.

Bake for 30 minutes. Cool the casseroles. Wrap them in foil. Label them, and freeze.

Thaw the lentil mixture in the refrigerator at least 24 hours before serving.

To Serve

Reheat the casserole for 20 minutes, or until heated through.

Black Beans and Rice

8 SERVINGS

2 cans black beans, drained (or use cooked dry beans)

20 ounces frozen corn

2 cups long grain rice, uncooked (white or brown)

32 ounces salsa (mild, medium, or hot)

3 cups tomato juice

½ teaspoon cumin

½ teaspoon oregano

2 cups grated cheddar cheese

In large bowl, combine all ingredients except cheese. Pour into two casserole dishes and bake, covered, at 375 degrees for 1 hour. Remove from oven. Cool, wrap, label, and freeze. Divide grated cheese into 2 small freezer bags, and attach the bags to the casseroles.

To Serve

Thaw. Sprinkle grated cheese over beans and rice; reheat at 350 degrees for 15 to 20 minutes, until cheese is melted and beans and rice are heated through.

Mexican Noodle Bake

SERVES 12

You can make this dish with cooked dried beans instead of the canned ones. Zucchini makes a nice addition, too, but slice and stir it in raw just before freezing to prevent sogginess.

2 tablespoons butter

2 cups chopped onions

2 cups chopped bell pepper

2 cups sliced celery

2 packages taco seasoning

2 (15-ounce) cans black beans, drained

2 (15-ounce) cans red kidney beans, undrained

32 ounces tomato sauce

32 ounces canned diced tomatoes

4 cups macaroni, cooked until just tender and drained

4 cups grated Cheddar cheese

Heat the butter in a large skillet or Dutch oven over medium heat, and sauté onions, bell pepper, and celery until just tender. Stir in the taco seasoning, beans, tomato sauce, and tomatoes. Reduce the heat to medium-low, and cook for 10 minutes. Stir in the macaroni noodles. Spread the mixture into two 9 × 13-inch casserole dishes. Wrap the casseroles in foil. Label them, and freeze. Divide grated cheese into 2 small freezer bags, and attach the bags to the casseroles.

To Serve

Thaw the mixture in the refrigerator at least 24 hours before serving. Preheat the oven to 375 degrees.

To serve, sprinkle grated cheese over top of the casserole. Bake, uncovered, for 45 minutes, or until the center is hot and the edges are bubbly.

Beef and Bean Burritos

SERVES 24

Submitted by Lynn Nelson

————◆◆◆————

4 tablespoons oil

2 onions, chopped

4 pounds ground beef

4 cloves garlic, minced

2 tablespoons chili powder

2 teaspoons cumin

Salt and pepper, to taste

16 ounces tomato sauce

62 ounces refried beans (canned or homemade)

24 flour tortillas

Heat the oil in a large skillet over medium heat. Sauté the onions until tender. Stir in the beef and garlic; cook until beef is no longer pink. Drain. Add chili powder, cumin, salt, and pepper. Stir in tomato sauce, and cook 5 minutes. Add the refried beans; cook and stir until well blended. Set aside to cool completely. Soften tortillas, if necessary, and place a small portion of the bean mixture in the center of each. Roll up, burrito-style, repeating until all the ingredients are used up. To freeze, place seam side down on a cookie sheet and freeze until firm. Wrap each individually and return to freezer.

To Serve

To serve, you can thaw first and then heat them, or heat the frozen burritos in the microwave.

Enchilada Pie

SERVES 15

This is so good! I could eat it every night, but I think the rest of my family would get a little tired of it after a while. Prepared according to instructions, this recipe makes a little layered "cake," but naming this recipe Enchilada Cake might be odd—I can almost hear people wondering what sort of frosting or icing to prepare for the cake. For easier and faster preparation, cut the tortillas into 1-inch pieces and just throw the whole mess into a casserole dish. It tastes the same, but it's just not quite as pretty.

2 tablespoons vegetable oil

3 pounds ground beef

3 onions, chopped

3 teaspoons salt (optional)

1 teaspoon pepper

3 tablespoons chili powder

24 ounces tomato sauce

18 corn tortillas, spread with butter and cut to fit into pans

12 ounces black olives, drained and chopped

3 cups shredded sharp Cheddar cheese

Heat the oil in a large skillet over medium heat. Sauté the ground beef and onion until browned. Add the seasonings and tomato sauce. In three 2-quart casseroles, alternate layers of tortillas, meat sauce, olives, and cheese. Add ½ cup water to each casserole. Wrap each tightly in foil. Label them, and freeze.

Thaw the casserole in the refrigerator at least 24 hours before serving. Preheat the oven to 400 degrees and bake for 20 minutes.

9
★ ★ ★

BREAKFASTS, LUNCHES, DESSERTS, AND MIXES

In many families, morning is a hectic and hurried time. Frequently, parents feel fortunate just to get everyone out the door fully dressed each day. Serve a hot breakfast every morning? Not a chance. Breakfast (if it's served at all) often consists of a toaster pastry and a quick glass of juice as the family runs out the door, racing headlong to work or school. Taking an hour or so on a weekend to prepare breakfast items for the freezer can take much of the insanity out of the weekday morning rush.

Many lunch items and desserts can be prepared for freezing. Sandwiches, slices of quiche, and pieces of cake can be placed directly into a lunchbox fully frozen and be completely thawed for eating by noon—all while keeping other items cold, too.

At the end of this section, I've included a recipe for a Multi-Purpose Baking Mix that's much like the boxed biscuit mixes you find at the grocery store. You can use this mix for preparing the recipes included after it: pancakes, waffles, biscuits, shortcakes, snack cakes, dumplings, and pizza crusts.

Breakfasts

Breakfast is an easy meal to prepare for the freezer. You can make sausage and egg casseroles, egg sandwiches, breakfast burritos, pancakes, French toast, waffles, muffins, quick breads, and baked oatmeal, for example. Having homemade breakfast items stashed away in your freezer cuts down on that early morning rush—plus, the meals are healthier and less expensive than stocking up on similar frozen items at the grocery store.

You can reheat many of these items quickly in the microwave. I've included simple recipes for waffles and pancakes in the Multi-Purpose Baking Mix section later in this chapter. To prepare waffles, pancakes, and French toast for freezing, cook until lightly browned, and be sure you don't overcook. To reheat, just pop them into the toaster as you would the boxed frozen waffles from the store; heating them in the toaster keeps them firm, rather than the limp and soggy result you often get when they're reheated in the microwave.

Holiday Breakfast Casserole

8 SERVINGS

6–8 slices bread (white or wheat), crusts removed

1 pound bulk sausage, cooked (or crumbled links)

6 ounces cheddar cheese, shredded

5 eggs

2 cups milk (or half-and-half)

1 teaspoon salt

1 teaspoon dry mustard

1 medium apple, peeled and diced

Lay bread in the bottom of an oblong 9 × 13-inch glass baking pan. Sprinkle the cooked sausage over bread. Sprinkle on the cheese. In a bowl, whip together the eggs, milk, salt, and dry mustard. Pour the egg mixture over the sausage-bread-cheese mixture in the pan and refrigerate overnight (for breakfast) or all day (for dinner). If freezing, skip the refrigeration instructions, wrap pan well, label, and freeze.

To Serve

Thaw completely. Bake in 350-degree oven for 35–40 minutes. Let set 10 minutes before serving.

Breakfast Sandwiches

SERVES 24

Note: Cook eggs inside greased canning rings to maintain a round shape.

2 dozen eggs

24 English muffins, toasted and buttered

24 regular bacon strips, cooked and drained

24 thin slices cheddar cheese

Scramble eggs in a large skillet, or fry eggs individually on a griddle. Put sandwiches together—1 English muffin, 1 egg, 1 strip of bacon cut in half, and 1 slice of cheese. Wrap each sandwich individually in a paper towel, and then place several sandwiches in large zip-top freezer bags. Label them, and freeze.

To Serve

Microwave on high for 1 to 2 minutes. Or thaw sandwiches, rewrap in foil, and bake at 400 degrees for 15 to20 minutes.

Substitutions

★ Fat-free egg substitute instead of eggs.

★ Large biscuits instead of English muffins. Be sure to undercook biscuits slightly, or they'll be too crumbly.

★ Canadian bacon (back bacon), ham slices, or cooked sausage patties instead of regular bacon slices.

Breakfast Burritos

MAKES 24 BURRITOS

12 eggs, beaten

1 pound bulk sausage or crumbled links, cooked

½ cup chunky salsa (mild, medium, or hot)

24 flour tortillas

2 cups shredded Cheddar cheese

Scramble eggs in large skillet until done; stir in cooked sausage and salsa. Warm tortillas in a microwave for 20 to 30 seconds, or until warm and softened. Place ½ cup egg mixture on half of the tortilla, roll the sides to the center, and roll the tortilla all the way up, burrito-style. Freeze the burritos in a single layer on a lightly greased cookie sheet. When fully frozen, wrap the burritos individually in foil, and store them in large zip-top freezer bags. Label them, and freeze.

To Serve

Unwrap foil-wrapped tortillas and warm them in microwave until heated through, about 2 minutes. Or thaw the burritos while they are still wrapped in foil, and bake them at 350 degrees for 10 minutes.

Additional Ingredient Options

★ 1 green pepper, diced

★ 6 potatoes, peeled, shredded, and fried until cooked through, or use hash browns

★ Slices of jalapeños

★ 1 to 2 cloves garlic, minced

★ 1 onion, diced

★ 1 tomato, peeled and chopped

★ 2 green onions, sliced, with tops

Mix-n-Match Quick Bread or Breakfast/ Snack Muffins

MAKES 2 LOAVES

3 cups all-purpose flour

3 teaspoons ground cinnamon

1 teaspoon baking soda

1 teaspoon salt

½ teaspoon baking powder

2 eggs

2 cups sugar

1 cup vegetable oil

2 cups Mix-n-Match Add-Ins (list follows)

1 tablespoon vanilla extract

1 cup chopped nuts or seeds

Mix-n-Match Add-Ins (one or more of the following, to equal 2 cups):

Apples, grated or chopped

Applesauce

Apricots, chopped

Bananas, mashed or chopped

Berries

Carrots, cooked and mashed or grated

Cherries, pitted and chopped

Coconut, grated

Cranberries, dry or raw, chopped

Dates or figs, pitted and finely chopped

Lemon juice, ½ cup

Marmalade (omit 1 cup sugar)

Mincemeat

Oranges, peeled and chopped

Orange juice, ½ cup

Peaches, fresh or canned, chopped

Pears, fresh or canned, chopped

Pineapple, crushed and well-drained

Prunes, pitted and chopped

Pumpkin purée, canned

Raisins, dark or golden

Rhubarb, finely chopped (add ½ cup more sugar)

Strawberries, well drained

Sweet potatoes or yams, cooked and mashed or grated and cooked

Zucchini, grated and well drained

For tasty Mix-n-Match combinations, try Carrot-Raisin-Walnut, Cranberry-Orange-Walnut or Pumpkin-Raisin-Sunflower Seed.

Directions

Preheat the oven to 325 degrees for bread, 375 degrees for muffins. Grease generously two 9-inch loaf pans or muffin tins. Bake for 1 hour for bread, or 15 minutes for muffins.

Sift together dry ingredients. In a separate bowl, beat the eggs, and stir in the sugar and oil, mixing well. Stir in the Mix-n-Match mix and vanilla. Fold in the dry ingredients; mix well. Stir in nuts. Spoon the batter into the prepared pans or muffin tins.

When cool, wrap the loaves in foil. Label them, and freeze. Wrap individual muffins in plastic wrap, and place them into large zip-top freezer bags. Muffins reheat well in a microwave. Serve with fresh fruit and juice for a light breakfast.

Lunches

Lunches at home can be prepared easily in advance. Use smaller servings of your regular dinner items for a lighter meal. And you can freeze and use many items to include in a brown-bag lunch.

Sandwiches

Sandwiches freeze nicely, and these fillings work well: cooked meat, tuna, sliced cheese, cheese spreads, hard-cooked egg yolks, and nut butters. Use day-old bread, and spread the bread lightly with butter or margarine to prevent the fillings from soaking into bread. Mixing jelly, mayonnaise, or salad dressing into the sandwich filling helps prevent soggy bread. Tomatoes and lettuce get limp when frozen, so add these after removing the sandwich from the freezer. Frozen sandwiches will thaw in lunch boxes in about 3 to 4 hours, staying fresh and at the same time, keeping other lunch-box foods cool.

Quiche

A cooked quiche can be frozen in individually wrapped slices, and for lunch, you can serve it warm, reheated in the microwave, or cold. Check out the Use-it-Up Quiche, Crustless Quiche, and Crab-and-Swiss Quiche recipes on pages 146–150.

Soups

The following is my favorite recipe for soup—it's simple, creative, delicious, and fun! My ten-year-old loves to choose the Mix-n-Match ingredients. This Mix-n-Match Soup recipe is adapted from the book *Cooking Ahead* by Mary Carney (used with permission).

Mix-n-Match Soup

8–10 SERVINGS

Base or broth—Choose one

> Tomato—one 12-ounce can tomato paste *plus* two 16-ounce cans tomatoes with juice (chopped) *plus* water, to equal 10 cups total

> Chicken/Turkey—10 cups broth *or* 4 bouillon cubes dissolved in 10 cups water

> Beef—10 cups broth *or* 4 bouillon cubes dissolved in 10 cups water

Protein—Choose one (1 pound or 2 cups, cooked)

> Ground beef, browned

> Leftover meatballs or meatloaf, chopped

> Cooked chicken or turkey, cut up

> Ham, cut up

> Dry beans, cooked (pintos, kidney, Great Northern, garbanzo, or a mixture of whatever is on hand)

> Lentils (raw)

> Frankfurters, sliced (any sausage or Kielbasa)

> Pepperoni, sliced

Grain—Choose one or two (2 cups)

> Rice, cooked (any variety)

> Barley, cooked

> Pasta, raw

Corn

Dumplings (add at end of cooking time)

Vegetables—Choose two or more
(1—2 cups—sliced, diced, or shredded)

Carrots	Turnips
Celery	Parsnips
Cabbage	Corn
Onion	Zucchini
Potatoes	Green pepper
Tomatoes	Peas or pea pods
Green beans	Cauliflower
Yellow "wax" beans	Broccoli
Whatever you have around	

Seasonings—Choose two to four (1—2 teaspoons each)

Basil	Oregano
Cayenne (dash)	Parsley
Chives	Rosemary
Cumin	Thyme
Garlic	Onion powder
Marjoram	

To Prepare Soup

Bring stock to boil in large stockpot or Dutch oven. Add all ingredients and salt and pepper, to taste; reduce heat and simmer 1 hour.

In Crockpot

Pour boiling stock and other ingredients into crockpot and simmer 8 to 12 hours or overnight on low setting.

Desserts

Many desserts lend themselves to advance preparation and freezing for later use. These include cakes, pies, cookies, brownies, dessert breads, muffins, cupcakes, and more. I'm only including a few dessert recipe in the book because most people already have their own family favorites, and most dessert items freeze well.

Frequently, commercial cake mixes go on sale at the grocery store. You can take advantage of the sale prices, stock up on mixes, prepare the cakes in advance, and either freeze them as layers ready to thaw and frost, or cut the cakes into serving-sized pieces, wrap each individually, and use them for snacks or desserts in lunch boxes.

Cakes

Layer, loaf, cupcake, angel, chiffon, sponge, and fruit: prepare all cakes as usual, bake them, and cool them. Freeze whole cakes, meal-sized portions, or slices. To prevent crushing, freeze whole cakes in boxes. Keep them in their wrappings to thaw in the refrigerator. For best results, freeze the cake and its frosting separately. Do not freeze any frosting containing egg whites. Be sure to frost frozen cake layers before they thaw, or frosting them will be difficult.

Candies

Fudge, divinity, brittle, taffy, and other homemade candies freeze well. Prepare the candies as usual, wrap each piece individually in plastic wrap, and package them in sturdy freezer containers before freezing them.

Cheesecake

Prepare as usual, then bake and cool. Freeze the cheesecake, uncovered, on a cookie sheet. Once it is solid, wrap it in foil, place it in a sturdy box to prevent crushing, and refreeze it.

Cookies

Baked cookies: Prepare as usual. Cool and package them with freezer paper or waxed paper between layers. Label them, and freeze.

Unbaked cookies: Prepare the dough as usual. Package, label it, and freeze. Thaw the dough in its wrapping in the refrigerator. Bake cookies as usual.

Doughnuts

Prepare as usual. Cool, and package them. Label them, and freeze.

Note: Yeast doughnuts freeze better than the cake type, and glaze soaks into doughnuts when frozen.

Muffins

Prepare and bake as usual. Cool, and package them in foil for reheating in the oven, or wrap them in plastic wrap for reheating in the microwave or for eating directly after thawing. Place individually wrapped muffins into zip-top freezer bags. Label them, and freeze. Thaw muffins in wrapping to eat cold, reheat unthawed in foil at 300 degrees for 20 minutes, or reheat unthawed in plastic wrap in the microwave for about 1 minute.

Pies

When preparing pies for the freezer, pour the unbaked pie filling into a lightly greased pie plate, freeze the pie until solid, pop the frozen pie-shaped filling out of the pie plate, and put it into a zip-top freezer bag. Label it, and freeze.

When it's time to prepare pies, just place the frozen pie-shaped filling into your piecrust. Thaw, and bake as usual. Easy as … pie!

Note: The filling for frozen fruit pies should be a bit thicker than usual.

Debi's Million-Dollar Chocolate Chip Cookies

MAKES 10 DOZEN COOKIES

I gave a neighbor some of these cookies one day, and he came running back over to my house with an amazed look in his eyes. "These are the best chocolate chip cookies I've ever had!" he exclaimed. "You could bake these and market them to local coffee shops!"

First, measure oatmeal. Then, blend the oatmeal into a fine powder in a mill or blender. This recipe can be halved, or you can freeze the extras for later.

2 cups butter

2 cups granulated sugar

2 cups brown sugar

4 eggs

2 teaspoons vanilla extract

4 cups all-purpose flour

2 teaspoons baking powder

2 teaspoons soda

1 teaspoon salt

5 cups blended oatmeal

24 ounces chocolate chips

1 (8-ounce) chocolate bar, grated

3 cups chopped walnuts

Preheat the oven to 375 degrees.

Cream together the butter and both sugars. Beat in the eggs and vanilla extract. Sift together the flour, baking powder, baking soda, and salt, and fold them into the egg mixture. Stir in the oats. Mix in chips, grated chocolate bar, and nuts. Roll the dough into balls, and place them 2 inches apart on a cookie sheet.

Bake for 10 minutes.

Recipes for the following dessert items are also included in this book:

★ Shortcake, see page 190

★ Snack Cake, see page 191

Multi-Purpose Baking Mix

This baking mix is similar to the boxed baking mixes you can purchase at the grocery store. This particular recipe contains dry milk, so you won't be adding more milk when preparing recipes, only water and eggs. Don't use this recipe as a one-to-one substitute for the big-name baking mixes, unless you substitute plain water for any added milk in their recipes. Note that instead of using whole-wheat flour, you can substitute all-purpose flour, cornmeal, or rolled oats. And if you use margarine instead of vegetable shortening, you must store the mix in the refrigerator or the margarine will turn rancid; you will need to stir it before use.

This baking mix can be used in the recipes for pancakes, waffles, biscuits, shortcakes, snack cakes, dumplings, and pizza crusts. Look for these recipes on the following pages.

4 cups all-purpose flour

4 cups whole-wheat flour

1⅓ cups nonfat dry milk

¼ cup baking powder

1 teaspoon salt

1½ cups vegetable shortening or margarine (do *not* use oil)

Stir dry ingredients together in a large mixing bowl until well mixed. Cut in the shortening or margarine until well mixed. Store in a covered container. If stored at room temperature, use within 1 month. Otherwise, store it in the refrigerator.

Pancakes

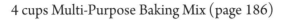

4 cups Multi-Purpose Baking Mix (page 186)

2 cups water

4 eggs, beaten

Stir together ingredients in a mixing bowl just until blended. The mixture will still be somewhat lumpy. Pour a scant ¼ cup onto a hot griddle. Cook until the edges are dry. Turn, and cook until golden. For fluffier pancakes, add 4 tablespoons lemon juice or vinegar, 8 teaspoons sugar, and 4 teaspoons baking powder. If you are preparing pancakes to freeze, undercook them slightly, freeze individually on a cookie sheet, and place the frozen pancakes into a freezer bag. Label them, and refreeze. To serve, reheat frozen pancakes in a toaster.

Waffles

4 cups Multi-Purpose Baking Mix (page 186)

1 ⅓ cups water

2 eggs

4 tablespoons vegetable oil

Preheat the waffle iron. Stir the ingredients in a mixing bowl until blended. Pour the batter onto the hot waffle iron, and cook according to manufacturer's directions. Freeze leftover waffles individually on a cookie sheet. Store the frozen waffles in a freezer bag. Label them, and freeze. To serve, reheat frozen waffles in a toaster.

Biscuits

MAKES 20 TWO-INCH BISCUITS

1 cup water

4 cups Multi-Purpose Baking Mix (page 186)

Preheat the oven to 400 degrees.

Add water to the Baking Mix, and stir about 20 times. Turn the dough out onto a lightly floured surface. Knead it with 10 to 15 strokes. Roll or pat it out to ¾-inch thick, and cut it with a biscuit cutter.

Bake on an ungreased pan or cookie sheet for 12 to 15 minutes. To freeze, place the biscuits in a freezer bag. Reheat them in a microwave.

Biscuit Variations

★ ¼ cup cooked and minced bacon

★ ⅔ cup grated cheese and ½ teaspoon garlic powder

★ ⅔ cup raisins and 2 tablespoons sugar

Shortcake

SERVES 12

4⅔ cups Multi-Purpose Baking Mix (page 186)

6 tablespoons sugar

6 tablespoons margarine or butter, melted

Preheat the oven to 425.

Stir the ingredients and 1 cup water in a large mixing bowl until a soft dough forms. Spread the batter into two ungreased 8-inch-square baking pans.

Bake for 15 to 20 minutes, or until golden brown. Slice into squares. Serve with sliced berries and whipped cream. For drop shortcakes: After stirring, drop the dough by ¼ cupfuls onto ungreased cookie sheets. Bake 10 to 12 minutes, or until golden brown.

Snack Cake

MAKES TWO 9-INCH-SQUARE CAKES

Topping:

½ cup all-purpose flour

¼ cup brown sugar

2½ tablespoons butter, softened

½ teaspoon ground cinnamon

Cake:

⅔ cup sugar

3 cups Multi-Purpose Baking Mix (page 186)

2 eggs

1 teaspoon vanilla extract

Preheat the oven to 350 degrees. Grease two 9-inch-square baking pans.

To make the topping, combine the topping ingredients, and mix with a pastry cutter or fork until crumbly. Set aside.

To make the cake, stir together the sugar with the Baking Mix in a large bowl. In a separate bowl, beat 1 cup water with the egg and vanilla until smooth and frothy. Stir the egg mixture into the Baking Mix, and beat until smooth. Pour the batter into the prepared pans, and sprinkle with the topping.

Bake for 25 minutes, or until firm in the center.

Dumplings

———————◆◆◆◆———————

2 cups Multi-Purpose Baking Mix (page 186)

⅔ cup water

Stir together the Baking Mix and water. Drop by heaping tablespoons into a boiling soup or stew. Cover the saucepan, and cook for 10 minutes. Remove the cover, and cook for 10 minutes more.

Pizza Crust

MAKES ONE 12-INCH PIZZA CRUST

This recipe isn't nearly as good as a pizza made with a yeast dough, but it'll do in a pinch. It's great if children want to try their hand at making pizza by themselves.

2 cups Multi-Purpose Baking Mix (page 186)

½ cup water

Preheat the oven to 425 degrees.

Stir ingredients together to make a soft dough. Knead it 6 to 8 times. Pat out the dough to a uniform thickness on a baking sheet; turn up the edges slightly. Add toppings, such as cheese, meat, vegetables, and sauce. Bake for 20 minutes, or until the edges are brown.

10
★ ★ ★

MONEY-SAVING TIPS AND IDEAS FOR GROCERIES

Many people who choose to try freezer-meal cooking do so with the intent of saving money on their grocery bills. Grocery shopping is one of the few semiflexible expense categories for most families. How much do you spend on groceries? $200 per week? $150? $100? Believe it or not, it's relatively simple to spend as little as $75 per week for a family of five.

When I first started investigating frugal food shopping, I was easily spending $600 per month on food and related items at the store. After learning and applying many of the following tips for shopping wisely and planning ahead, I've been able to reduce our family's food bill considerably—often spending as little as $200 per month for groceries (excluding toiletries, cleaning supplies, paper products, and similar products).

Probably the greatest help to our family's financial picture has been establishing a budget. Now, don't start hyperventilating and tune me out. I realize the B-word does strange things to people. If the word "budget" makes you sweat and turn purple, try substituting the term "spending plan." For some reason, a spending plan is less psychologically threatening to many people than a b-b-b-b-b-budget.

The spending plan our family implemented is also known as the Envelope System. It's easy and relatively painless, and it works. This simple plan did more to turn around our financial picture than any other single change we've made in our spending habits.

First, we figured out how much money we needed each month for the different expense categories (food, clothing, gasoline, bus fare, coffee at work, and others), and placed that amount of cash (yes, the green paper stuff!) into separately labeled envelopes. We then had a concrete visual aid to show us exactly how much money we had left to spend in each category, and we clearly saw how borrowing money from one envelope left us less money in another. And once the money's gone, it's gone.

The Envelope System is perfect for people who tend to think that if there's a positive balance in the checkbook, they can keep writing checks. Shopping with cash in hand also tends to make people more aware of the reality of the money they're spending. It feels more "real" to part with a handful of ten-dollar bills than just writing out a check for the same eighty dollars.

My husband and I learned this simple budgeting trick from the old Marlo Thomas television show, *That Girl*. In our case, life imitated art. (Maybe claiming *That Girl* as art is stretching the analogy a bit too far.)

There's no magic formula to living within your means, whatever those means might be. I've known people living beneath the poverty line who never go into debt and never have outstanding bills. I've also seen families who live in the grandest homes in town struggling to stay afloat each month due to overspending. Whether yours is a financially strapped single-income family, a household headed by a single working mother or father, or a double-income family with mounting consumer debt, you can probably use a good dose of reality in the financial area of your life.

The following one hundred easy tips should help you gain some control over your grocery bills and food-related spending.

General Money-Saving Food Tips

1) Go grocery shopping with cash only. Leave your credit cards, debit cards, and checkbook at home. Keep a running total of the groceries in your cart as you shop. If you overspend your grocery budget, you'll need to put something back on the shelf or shop for less-expensive alternatives.

2) Avoid prepackaged items and convenience foods. Homemade alternatives are almost always cheaper.

3) Think of meat as a side dish or condiment, and serve it in smaller portions.

4) Eat meat less frequently.

5) Make friends with a hunter or fisherman who is willing to share his bounty.

6) At mealtimes, serve everyone a single glass of juice or milk. Make refills plain water.

7) Drink water only; this keeps food costs down if your budget is really tight. Be sure your children are getting adequate servings of dairy products in other forms if you don't serve milk with meals.

8) Make your own seasoning mixes.

9) Make dessert a special treat, rather than a daily occurrence.

10) Bake cakes from scratch. It's much cheaper and often as easy as using a packaged mix or purchasing prepared cakes from the bakery.

11) Buy popcorn. It's one of the least expensive snacks you'll find.

12) Buy large bags of pretzels, chips, and other snack items on sale. Re-package them into small zip-top bags to pop into lunches.

13) Learn to cook dried beans.

14) Make your own bread crumbs and croutons from leftover bread and crusts.

15) Use reconstituted powdered milk in baked goods and any recipes that call for milk.

16) Use butter and margarine wrappers to grease baking pans and foil. Store your butter wrappers in a large zip-top bag in the freezer, pulling one out when needed.

17) Make a regular breakfast on Sundays, and serve your main meal in the afternoon after church. Then, use up the week's leftovers for a light evening meal.

18) Raise your own homegrown fruit, such as raspberries. Raspberry bushes make a nice hedge to edge your yard. Rather than planting ornamental shade trees, plant fruit trees, such as apple, pear, peach, or cherry.

19) Grow salad vegetables in containers on your front porch or deck, if you don't have room for a garden in your yard.

20) Grow herbs easily indoors in small pots near a bright window.

21) Breast-feed your baby. Mother's milk is healthy and free, and free is the best price of all!

22) Make your own baby food. Any foods can be quickly chopped or blended in a food processor or blender. Scoop homemade baby foods into ice cube trays and freeze. Pop out the frozen food cubes and place them into large freezer bags. When it's time to feed baby, take out the amount of cubes you'll need, heat, and serve.

23) Invite people over for an evening of light snacks and desserts when entertaining at home. If you must serve dinner, make it potluck. You can provide the main dish, drinks, plates, and silverware, and ask each guest to bring a salad, dessert, or side dish.

24) When dining out, go at lunchtime or breakfast rather than dinner. Luncheon menus are often half the price of dinner menus, but many times offer the same general selections.

25) Order water to drink when dining out. Ask for a lemon or lime wedge to make it special.

26) Find out if there's a SHARE or similar food co-op program in your area. SHARE is a food buying co-op where you get a box or bag full of food valued at $40 to $50 for only $17 plus two hours community service. (The community service can even be something like working in a church nursery, volunteering for the PTA, helping a shut-in neighbor, or teaching Sunday school.)

Saving Strategies for Grocery Shopping

27) Set your grocery budget, and then make up your menus and shopping list to fit your budget, rather than the other way around.

28) Set price goals for each meal, which is one simple approach to meal planning. For example: Breakfast price goal = $0.50 per person per meal; dinner price goal = $3 to $4 per meal total. If you know you can make a home-cooked meal for only $4, you will be less tempted to make a quick (and expensive!) trip to the local drive-thru window.

29) Prepare a master shopping list of items you buy regularly. Add additional items as needed.

30) Check store flyers always for their weekly specials and private coupons.

31) Forget impulse buying! Stick to your shopping list religiously.

32) Take a calculator with you to the grocery store for comparing unit prices and to keep a running total of purchases.

33) Keep a list of sale prices of various foods you buy regularly. When you see something on sale, you can check your price list to see if it's really a good buy or not. If it is, stock up. It's so important to know your prices. Just because an item is advertised as a "sale item" doesn't mean it's necessarily a good buy.

34) Avoid buying nonfood items at the grocery store. You can buy items like housewares, greeting cards, over-the-counter medicines, toiletries, etc. elsewhere for less money.

35) Avoid shopping when you're hungry. You're more likely to make impulse buys when your stomach is grumbling.

36) Try not to shop with children. "Helpers" tend to add more items to your grocery cart while also distracting you from the task at hand.

37) Take your time shopping. It pays to examine labels, check products' cost per serving, compare brands, and make other cost-cutting efforts.

38) Be sure to look on the lowest and highest shelves for bargains. Stores often place the highest-priced items at eye level.

39) Avoid buying an item stacked at the end of an aisle unless you're certain it's on sale. Often, stores will display their sale items with expensive nonsale items. For example, spaghetti sauce may be on sale, but the store's most expensive brand of pasta or Parmesan cheese may be displayed with the discounted sauce.

40) Check to see if your local grocery store offers any preferred shopper programs for loyal shoppers.

41) Shop at a local farmers' market.

42) Use coupons for items and brands you normally buy.

43) Check the expiration dates on your coupons frequently.

44) Give the cashier your coupons up front; you'll be less likely to forget about the coupons later on. Or carry your coupons in an envelope along with your shopping list.

45) Buy in bulk whenever possible, but check unit prices to make sure you're really getting a bargain.

46) Join a warehouse shopping club for your bulk purchases, but once

again, remember to keep track of unit pricing. This is a time when keeping a price list of items you frequently buy can really pay off. You'll be amazed how many times items at the warehouse store aren't really cheaper per pound than the sale prices at the supermarket.

47) Contact the manufacturer directly, and save even more money if you buy in bulk often.

48) Watch closely as the cashier rings up your groceries with an electronic scanner. Occasionally, the scanner will come up with an incorrect price. Some stores will give you incorrectly scanned items for free!

49) Ask the store manager if you can browse through their dented-can collection—usually sold for pennies on the dollar. Stores often sell diapers and other products at a discount if the bags have been ripped or opened.

50) Check store entrances for special flyers, and don't forget to look in local newspapers for additional coupons.

51) Get a rain check if an advertised item is out of stock.

52) Return any spoiled item.

53) Use cloth kitchen towels and napkins, laundering them frequently, because paper products can run up the grocery bill.

Food Purchasing Specifics

54) Give store brands a try. The prices are often 20 to 50 percent below similar name-brand products. You won't know which store brands are good unless you're willing to take a chance and try them. If you find a tasty, high-quality store brand or generic product, you'll save money. Still, remember to compare prices. The sale price of a brand-name product will sometimes be lower than the regular price of a store brand.

55) Buy whole birds if you really want to save money, and use the bones for soup to stretch your purchase further. Boneless and skinless chicken is very expensive.

56) Check with local farmers to see if they sell beef. You can often purchase half a cow for less than $1.00 per pound. This includes steaks, roasts, and more, not just ground beef.

57) Buy for the lowest cost available with the least amount of packaging when purchasing basic grocery supplies (rice, beans, pasta, flour, oatmeal, vegetable oil, tuna, and others).

58) Buy spices in bulk.

59) Buy cheese in large quantities when it goes on sale. Grate the cheese, and freeze it in zip-top freezer bags. To use, just take out the amount of cheese you need, and keep the rest frozen.

60) Purchase plain frozen vegetables, and make your own seasonings and sauce rather than buying expensive frozen vegetables in a ready-made sauce.

61) Buy large bags of fresh potatoes, and store potatoes in a cool, dark place.

62) Buy produce in season and on sale.

63) Watch for sales on bulk ground meats. Divide the meat into one-pound batches, and freeze in individual freezer bags.

64) Find out when your store's meat department marks down meats. If the store is running a sale on ground beef for $1.00 per pound, and then the department marks down their meat by 50 percent on a particular day, you may be able to purchase packages for as little as $0.50 per pound.

65) Ask the department managers what time of day they mark down bakery, dairy, and produce items for a quick sale.

66) Buy large quantities of bread, rolls, and other baked goods at bakery

outlet stores, and freeze the bread items. You can often find top-quality multigrain breads for as little as four loaves for $1.00. The usual outlet price in my area is around $0.50 per loaf for name-brand multigrain breads. Compare that to paying $2 to $3 for the very same bread in the supermarket.

67) Buy grains, flours, sugars, and dried beans from a grocery warehouse or food co-op.

68) When purchasing prebagged produce, such as apples, oranges, and potatoes, weigh several bags to find the heaviest one. A five-pound bag of apples has a minimum of five pounds, but could actually contain a pound or two more. This will lower your price per pound.

Breakfast Ideas

69) Serve oatmeal (not the instant kind) as your regular breakfast meal. If you buy in bulk or use store brands, you usually can't find a less expensive breakfast. Dress oatmeal up with raisins, brown sugar, cinnamon, jam, bits of fruit, or whatever makes it special for your family.

70) Consider other inexpensive breakfast ideas: muffins, pancakes, waffles, French toast, cream of wheat, and homemade egg sandwiches.

71) Use store brands or homemade products for inexpensive syrups.

72) Make a big batch of pancakes or other economical breakfast meal options, allowing extras for afternoon snacking, when making Saturday brunch.

73) Buy large boxes of breakfast cereal, which are often much cheaper per serving than small convenience sizes. The least expensive form of cereal to purchase is usually packaged in plastic bags rather than cardboard boxes.

74) Buy juices as frozen concentrate, saving about half the cost of bottled juice.

75) Serve breakfast juice in small juice glasses rather than larger beverage glasses. It really makes the juice stretch.

76) Learn to make omelets. They're economical; a good source of protein; and a great way to use up leftover meats, vegetables, and cheeses.

77) Use rice (brown or converted), barley, and other whole grains that can be cooked and eaten just like oatmeal.

Lunch Tips

78) Use leftovers to make homemade frozen TV dinners you can take to work and warm in the microwave.

79) Pack your own lunch for work. Most people spend at least $5 per workday on food-related items at work (lunch, pop, coffee, snacks, etc.). Bringing lunches, snacks, sodas, and a thermos of coffee from home can easily save $100 per month—or $1,200 per year!

80) Pack lunches for your kids to take to school, rather than purchasing school lunches.

81) Remember that sandwiches made with the old standbys, peanut butter and jelly, are still a hit with kids today.

82) Purchase lunch meat at the deli counter, where it is usually cheaper per pound than prepackaged containers.

83) Pack reusable thermos bottles filled with juice or milk instead of buying individual disposable juice boxes.

84) Pack your own gelatin, pudding, applesauce, and fruit-cup snacks for school lunches in small, plastic, and reusable containers.

85) Purchase lunch-box snacks and desserts at the bakery thrift store and freeze them.

86) For dessert, pack a frozen slice of homemade cake or a brownie, treats you can bake and slice ahead of time. The frozen treats can go directly into the lunch box and will be defrosted by noon.

87) Keep lunches at home simple: sandwiches, soups, salads, fresh fruit, sliced cheese, or crackers.

88) Make your own homemade soups from leftovers for lunch. You can also pack the soup in thermos containers for lunches away from home.

Dinner Meal Stretchers

89) Stretch each whole chicken purchase into three meals (I've heard this idea referred to as "rubber chicken"—you just keep stretching it out!). Use the joint pieces for a meal of barbecued, fried, or baked chicken. Cut up the breast meat, and use it in a casserole or a skillet meal. Save the bones and any leftover meat for homemade chicken soup.

90) Check if ground turkey is less expensive than other ground meats in your area. If this is the case, substitute ground turkey in your ground beef recipes.

91) Substitute turkey ham and turkey sausages in recipes.

92) Keep ingredients on hand for several quick and easy meals. When time is scarce, you won't be as tempted to run out to the local drive-thru for a fast meal. Freezer meals help with this, too.

93) Serve breakfast for dinner occasionally. Even when prepared in a big way, breakfast is one of the most economical meals to make. At our house, we rarely have time for a big breakfast of pancakes, eggs, bacon and fruit in the morning, so it's a special treat to have a meal like that for dinner.

94) Remember that omelets are fun and economical dinner meals, too.

You can serve them with almost any side dishes (not just breakfast-type items).

95) Stretch your meat by adding oatmeal or dry bread crumbs to ground meat. Flavor the meat with herbs.

96) Stretch budgets with vegetable and noodle casseroles with meat.

97) Remember that turkey is usually a better value per pound than chicken. Substitute cooked turkey in your cooked chicken recipes, and use leftover turkey for sandwiches and casseroles.

98) Remember that larger turkeys have a higher proportion of meat to bone, making them more economical.

99) Save electricity or gas by cooking several items in the oven at one time.

100) Cook up a big pot of soup for dinner one night during the weekend, and you'll be set with several easy lunches for the week.

★ ★ ★

APPENDIX A:
FOODS THAT DON'T FREEZE WELL

1) Mayonnaise separates. It can be used in limited amounts if mixed with other ingredients in a sauce or casserole.

2) Sour cream becomes watery, but you can also use it in the same ways as mayonnaise.

3) Fried foods lose crispness and become soggy.

4) Soft cheeses, such as cream cheese, often become watery, so don't use them alone. They can be used mixed into recipes, however.

5) Potatoes cooked in soups and stews can become mushy and dark. Save potatoes to add raw just before freezing, making sure to cover them completely with soup or stew liquid.

6) Cake icings made with egg whites, cream fillings, soft frostings, and custard- or cream-filled pies don't freeze well.

7) Cooked egg whites become tough and rubbery.

Foods that Change in the Freezer

1) Raw vegetables lose crispness, but can be cooked or used for soups, stews, and casserole-type recipes.

2) Gravies and fat-based sauces may separate and will need to be recombined after thawing. Stir during reheating to recombine.

3) Thickened sauces may need to be thinned after freezing; stir in a small amount of milk or broth.

4) Some seasonings can change flavor during freezing, such as onion, garlic, black pepper, cloves, cinnamon, nutmeg, vanilla, almond and mint extracts, thyme, rosemary, basil, dill, and sage. For best flavor, add herbs and other seasonings when you reheat the meal.

5) Heavy cream can be frozen, but it won't whip when thawed.

6) Milk can be frozen for drinking, but will often separate and need to be shaken or stirred to recombine.

7) Vegetables, pastas, and grains are softer after thawing and reheating. Undercook these before freezing. If you're adding noodles to soups, either add the raw noodles after thawing so they will cook during the reheating process, or add raw noodles to the soup after cooling and just before freezing.

8) Cheeses often change texture in the freezer. Many hard cheeses become crumbly; these are good for use in recipes but not for slicing. Hard cheeses freeze best if grated before freezing.

APPENDIX B: RECIPE EQUIVALENTS

Recipes will often call for two cups of diced onions or three cups of grated cheese. This makes it difficult to know how many whole onions to buy, or what quantity of block cheese to add to your shopping list. Following are approximate equivalents for common recipe ingredients:

1 medium onion = 1 cup, diced

1 medium green pepper = 1 cup, diced

3 ounces fresh mushrooms = 1 cup, sliced

2 large celery ribs = 1 cup, sliced or diced

2 cups margarine or butter = 1 pound

1 medium clove garlic = 1 teaspoon, minced

1 medium apple = 1 cup, chopped

4 to 5 cups cooked noodles = 8 ounces, uncooked

8 ounces uncooked spaghetti = 4 cups, cooked

1 pound raw ground beef = 2½ cups, browned

1 medium tomato = 1 cup, chopped

1 pound flour = 3½ cups

8 slices bacon = ½ cup, crumbled

4 ounces (¼ pound) cheese = 1 cup, grated

1 pound ham = 3 cups, cubed

3- to 4-pound whole chicken = 4 cups cooked meat

Equivalent Measures

1 tablespoon = 3 teaspoons, ½ fluid ounce

2 tablespoons = 1 fluid ounce

4 tablespoons = ¼ cup

8 tablespoons = ½ cup

16 tablespoons = 1 cup

1 cup = ½ pint, 8 fluid ounces

2 cups = 1 pint

4 cups = 1 quart

4 quarts = 1 liquid gallon

APPENDIX C:
TIPS FOR SINGLES

1) Freeze leftovers in individual serving sizes when you cook a meal with more than one serving. Most foods can be frozen in single servings and reheated in the microwave.

2) Freeze individual portions of baked chicken, quiche, pizza, and other foods, in sandwich bags. Then pack the bagged portions into one large freezer bag, and label, date, and freeze them. If you have company, just pull out the number of individual servings you'll need from the bag and reheat.

3) Prepare things in advance that can be used in more than one way: meatballs, stew, chili, spaghetti sauce, and other foods.

4) Save time and effort by cooking similar recipes at once. If you purchase a whole chicken, you can make several meals from that one purchase: chicken soup, baked chicken, chicken tacos, and others.

5) Look in restaurant supply stores for individual aluminum foil containers or freezer-to-microwave pans.

6) Try a cooperative effort. Find a single friend (or two!) to cook with and divide up the frozen meals.

★ ★ ★

APPENDIX D:
REDUCING FAT IN RECIPES

1) Substitute nonfat sour cream or nonfat plain yogurt for regular sour cream.

2) Substitute an equal amount of yogurt cheese for cream cheese. To make yogurt cheese, place plain yogurt into the center of a piece of cheesecloth or a coffee filter, and let the liquid (whey) drain out into a bowl. You can save the whey to use in making soup stock or to replace the liquids used in bread and other recipes.

3) Remember that cream soups are high in fat. If you want creaminess, use nonfat evaporated milk, a perfect substitute for cream in recipes. Mix nonfat evaporated milk with lightly cooked mushrooms, celery, or chicken (with broth) to make your own flavored cream soups. Instead of cream-of-whatever soup, you can also double or triple the amount of vegetables called for in the recipe and then purée half the vegetables in a blender or food processor.

4) Remember that if a recipe calls for sautéing in butter, margarine, or oil, you can cook them instead in a microwave: place the chopped vegetables into a covered and vented microwave-safe bowl with a

small amount of water or vegetable broth. Microwave on high until softened.

5) Use nonstick cookware to dramatically reduce the amount of fat and oils used in cooking.

6) Use the strongest flavor cheese you can buy, and then use half the recommended amount. If a recipe calls for 1 cup medium Cheddar, try ½ cup sharp Cheddar instead.

7) Use homemade vegetable stock instead of chicken or beef stock. Save all the peelings and end pieces from vegetables. Keep a container or bag in the refrigerator or freezer just for peelings. When the container's full, place the peelings into a crockpot or large stockpot along with some sliced onion, celery, carrots, garlic, and herbs, and cook on low heat all day. Strain out the vegetables, and you'll have a tasty, healthy vegetable stock.

8) To remove the fat from homemade chicken stock, let the stock cool and then refrigerate it for several hours. The fat will rise to the surface and solidify, so you can easily skim it off with a spoon.

9) Drain fried ground beef thoroughly in a colander and then rinse it well with hot water.

10) Boil, rather than fry, ground beef. Bring a large stockpot full of water to a boil. Place the raw ground beef into the boiling water, stirring to separate. Boil until meat is cooked through. Drain. You can save the cooking water and chill it so you can skim off the surface fat. Use the ground beef cooking water in soup.

11) Remember that in sweet baked goods, you can use an equal amount of applesauce or prune purée in place of oil.

APPENDIX E:
CREATIVE USES FOR FREEZER MEALS

Freezer Meal Baby Shower

I believe one of the greatest gifts for a new mom is a freezer full of home-cooked food—especially for a mother with older children at home. This type of baby shower works best if it's hosted before the baby's arrival. Have each guest bring one or two favorite frozen meals to send home with the mom-to-be. You can also include frozen side dishes and desserts.

Meals for Others

Many individuals and churches provide home-cooked meals for the sick, new moms, families in crisis, and others. I've found by having a handy supply of freezer meals, I can easily provide a meal for someone who's going through a difficult time. Often, I will purposely prepare a couple of extra meals each month for giving to others. A church I attended when my first baby was born had a ministry called Moms Helping Moms. One of the main aspects of the Moms' ministry was to provide meals for the new moms in the church. The freezer full of food I received after giving birth to a premature baby was one of the greatest things ever done for me.

Cooking with a Friend

Many freezer-meal cooks find that cooking with a partner can be a lot of fun. Some things you need to take into consideration when choosing a cooking partner are: family size, how well you get along, basic tastes in food, and special diets. You can also benefit by sharing cookware, appliances, and knowledge. Try to get together in person to do your planning session. Share a dozen of your respective families' favorite tried-and-true recipes. Try to find ten recipes you can both agree on, and prepare three meals of each recipe for a month's worth of food. Go through the regular Frozen Assets planning and preparation steps together. It helps if you divide the various duties beforehand. Maybe one of you can do the shopping one month while the other takes care of baby-sitting duties. And one could prepare chicken meals while the other prepares ground-beef meals. Be sure to label the frozen meals with each person's name while you're preparing the meals for freezing. One potential difficulty of cooking with someone else is a lack of freezer space during cooking day. You might want to plan on cooking at the home with the most available freezer space. Also, have several picnic coolers handy for transporting frozen meals to your home.

Group Meal Exchange

If you know a group of people interested or experienced in cooking for the freezer, you can arrange a group meal exchange. This is sometimes referred to as a "freezer potluck." If you have ten people in your group, everyone would prepare ten family-sized portions of one recipe. Then, the group would get together every ten days to exchange meals. A meal exchange works best if done with similar-sized families with similar tastes. Each member of the group could also prepare thirty family-sized portions of a single recipe and then exchange meals only once a month (eating the same meal three times during the month). To discover meals that most people in the group would like, ask each group member what their three family favorite meals are, or what they frequently serve to company. This potluck technique works well for the people I know who have tried it—each family gets a variety of frozen meals without one person having to do all the cooking.

This method of cooking for the freezer would also be helpful for groups of singles. Singles would only need to prepare thirty single-serving meals.

Organizing a frozen meal exchange for members of a local senior center would be a great way to ensure that single seniors are eating properly.

APPENDIX F:
RECOMMENDED RESOURCES

Freezer Meal Books

★ *Cooking Ahead,* by Mary Carney

As a homeschooling mother of four, minister's wife, frequent seminar speaker, and freelance writer, Mary Carney has depended on her *Cooking Ahead* techniques to simplify her busy life.

★ *Once-a-Month Cooking*, by Mary-Beth Lagerborg and Mimi Wilson

This book revolutionized the way I feed my family. Although I found the recipes to be too expensive for my limited grocery budget, I discovered that by applying their methods to my own recipes, I've saved substantial time, energy, and money each month.

★ *Dinner's in the Freezer,* by Jill Bond

★ *30 Day Gourmet,* by Nanci Slagle

Colorful three-ring binder with recipes arranged according to main protein group. *30 Day Gourmet* emphasizes sharing your big cooking day with a friend, and includes charts and planning sheets to simplify cooking with someone else. This manual must be purchased directly from the authors.

Cooking–Related Books

★ *Cheapskate in the Kitchen,* by Mary Hunt

Learn to prepare delicious gourmet meals for a fraction of the cost of restaurant dining. (I contributed several recipes to this book.)

★ *Eat Healthy for $50 a Week: Feed Your Family Nutritious, Delicious Meals for Less (Paperback),* by Rhonda Barfield

Feed your family nutritious delicious meals for less. Yes, it really is possible to feed your family healthy meals for $50 per week. Barfield shows you how.

★ *Mix-n-Match Recipes,* by Deborah Taylor-Hough

Simple and creative recipes using common ingredients—a great way to use up leftovers. Soup, quiche, skillet meals, casseroles, dessert breads, and more.

★ *More-With-Less Cookbook,* by Doris Janzen Longacre

The classic, thoughtful cookbook published by the Mennonites—every kitchen needs this book on the shelf.

Frugal Living

Many people choose freezer-meal methods for the money-saving advantages. Here are some more resources down the frugal-living path.

★ *Simple Living,* by Deborah Taylor-Hough

A collection of helpful money-saving tips, ideas, and resources. Putting just one of these ideas to action could easily save you the cost of this booklet.

★ *Miserly Moms Living on One Income in a Two-Income Economy* by Jonni McCoy

Practical book for living well on a limited budget. McCoy shares her "Eleven Miserly Guidelines" that will help you trim expenses on everything from groceries to household cleaners. Lots of helpful recipes and tips. Includes a chapter on bulk cooking.

Blank Calendar for Cooking Plans

MONDAY	TUESDAY	WEDNESDAY	THURSDAY	FRIDAY	SATURDAY	SUNDAY

Blank Calendar for Cooking Plans

MONDAY	TUESDAY	WEDNESDAY	THURSDAY	FRIDAY	SATURDAY	SUNDAY

RECIPES

NAME OF DISH _____   SERVINGS _____

NOTES

INGREDIENTS:

_____
_____
_____
_____
_____
_____
_____
_____
_____
_____

PREPARATION INSTRUCTIONS:

_____
_____
_____
_____
_____

FREEZING INSTRUCTIONS:

_____
_____
_____
_____

THAWING AND HEATING INSTRUCTIONS:

_____
_____
_____
_____

RECIPES

NAME OF DISH _____ SERVINGS _____

NOTES

INGREDIENTS:

_____
_____
_____
_____
_____
_____
_____
_____
_____
_____

PREPARATION INSTRUCTIONS:

_____
_____
_____
_____

FREEZING INSTRUCTIONS:

_____
_____
_____
_____

THAWING AND HEATING INSTRUCTIONS:

_____
_____
_____
_____

RECIPES

NAME OF DISH _____   SERVINGS _____

NOTES

INGREDIENTS:

_____
_____
_____
_____
_____
_____
_____
_____
_____

PREPARATION INSTRUCTIONS:

_____
_____
_____
_____
_____

FREEZING INSTRUCTIONS:

_____
_____
_____
_____

THAWING AND HEATING INSTRUCTIONS:

_____
_____
_____
_____

RECIPES

NAME OF DISH _____ SERVINGS _____

NOTES

INGREDIENTS:

_____
_____
_____
_____
_____
_____
_____
_____
_____
_____

PREPARATION INSTRUCTIONS:

_____
_____
_____
_____
_____

FREEZING INSTRUCTIONS:

_____
_____
_____
_____

THAWING AND HEATING INSTRUCTIONS:

_____
_____
_____
_____

RECIPES

NAME OF DISH _____ SERVINGS _____

NOTES

INGREDIENTS:

_____
_____
_____
_____
_____
_____
_____
_____
_____

PREPARATION INSTRUCTIONS:

_____
_____
_____
_____
_____

FREEZING INSTRUCTIONS:

_____
_____
_____
_____

THAWING AND HEATING INSTRUCTIONS:

_____
_____
_____
_____

RECITES

NAME OF DISH _____ SERVINGS _____

NOTES

INGREDIENTS:

_____
_____
_____
_____
_____
_____
_____
_____
_____
_____

PREPARATION INSTRUCTIONS:

_____
_____
_____
_____
_____

FREEZING INSTRUCTIONS:

_____
_____
_____
_____

THAWING AND HEATING INSTRUCTIONS:

_____
_____
_____
_____

RECIPES

NAME OF DISH _____   SERVINGS _____

NOTES

INGREDIENTS:

_____
_____
_____
_____
_____
_____
_____
_____
_____
_____

PREPARATION INSTRUCTIONS:

_____
_____
_____
_____
_____

FREEZING INSTRUCTIONS:

_____
_____
_____
_____

THAWING AND HEATING INSTRUCTIONS:

_____
_____
_____
_____

Blank Shopping List

CANNED

- [ ] _____
- [ ] _____
- [ ] _____
- [ ] _____
- [ ] _____
- [ ] _____
- [ ] _____
- [ ] _____
- [ ] _____

MEATS

- [ ] _____
- [ ] _____
- [ ] _____
- [ ] _____
- [ ] _____
- [ ] _____
- [ ] _____
- [ ] _____
- [ ] _____

GRAINS / PASTAS

- [ ] _____
- [ ] _____
- [ ] _____
- [ ] _____
- [ ] _____
- [ ] _____
- [ ] _____
- [ ] _____

DAIRY

- [ ] _____
- [ ] _____
- [ ] _____
- [ ] _____
- [ ] _____
- [ ] _____
- [ ] _____
- [ ] _____

PRODUCE

- [ ] _____
- [ ] _____
- [ ] _____
- [ ] _____
- [ ] _____
- [ ] _____
- [ ] _____

BAKERY

- [ ] _____
- [ ] _____
- [ ] _____
- [ ] _____
- [ ] _____
- [ ] _____
- [ ] _____

FREEZER BAGS, FOILS, ALUMINUM TRAYS

- [ ] _____
- [ ] _____
- [ ] _____
- [ ] _____
- [ ] _____
- [ ] _____
- [ ] _____
- [ ] _____
- [ ] _____
- [ ] _____

MISC.

- [ ] _____
- [ ] _____
- [ ] _____
- [ ] _____
- [ ] _____
- [ ] _____
- [ ] _____
- [ ] _____
- [ ] _____
- [ ] _____
- [ ] _____
- [ ] _____
- [ ] _____
- [ ] _____
- [ ] _____

FROZEN

- [ ] _____
- [ ] _____
- [ ] _____
- [ ] _____
- [ ] _____
- [ ] _____
- [ ] _____
- [ ] _____
- [ ] _____

STAPLES

- [ ] _____
- [ ] _____
- [ ] _____
- [ ] _____
- [ ] _____
- [ ] _____
- [ ] _____
- [ ] _____

FREEZING SUPPLIES

- [ ] _____
- [ ] _____
- [ ] _____
- [ ] _____
- [ ] _____
- [ ] _____
- [ ] _____

RECIPE INDEX BY MAIN INGREDIENT

ABOUT THE AUTHOR

Deborah Taylor-Hough is a freelance writer who runs a household and home-schools three children while balancing a limited budget and maintaining many outside interests.